RAMA

American Buddha

RAMA, AMERICAN BUDDHA

Published By
American Buddha, Inc.
New York, New York
www.americanbuddha.com

First Edition
Printed in the United States of America

ISBN 0-615-11517-9

For Rama,
with gratitude

Forward

The following stories are individuals' personal experiences with Rama and were submitted by his students for this publication. They were compiled by editors, who were also his students, into this book.

-The Editors

Introduction

Rama is an Icon of Enlightenment. There are no words to describe him, no commentaries to give his teachings justice. His life was an ongoing poem, a dynamic mandala of joy, pain, beauty, genius, humor and commitment. He extended his Enlightenment to all who came into contact with him. He provided a stage, protected and lit up by his own aura, for his students to evolve, grow, learn and live through their many mistakes, or as he would call them, *lessons*.

He gave ceaselessly, living the bodhisattva ideal, ready to do whatever it took to assist his students in their Enlightenment process. Through my experience of studying with him for eighteen years, it seems to me that he was the Incarnation of Avalokiteshvara, the manifestation of perfect compassion. We, his students, could not understand his ways, his methods, but all agree they were effective, and they were motivated by the highest love. If we tried, transformation was inevitable. Rama challenged, cajoled, graced, pushed, pulled, entertained, prodded and amused us out of our complacency. It was not always comfortable, hearing the truth, facing the illusions that he shattered one by one. Most students, through honest examination, would admit some form of anger toward Rama. It is the anger that comes with the imminent annihilation of ego. Nothing, however, stopped Rama from his mission. He embodied the meaning of the word Guru, *Dispeller of Darkness*. He was a twentieth century front-end to Enlightenment, in the tradition of his predecessors, Ramakrishna, Padmasambhava, Bodhi Dharma and Shakyamuni Buddha.

Rama taught in archetypes. He took his students to the source of the thing he wanted to teach and showed us the inner structural underpinnings. He insisted on school or books for the mundane lessons, and would then take us to the heart of whatever he was teaching to provide the most advanced understanding. For instance, in meditation, he showed us the *source* of computer programming, giving us an expansive view, beyond the superficial book that was necessary for impeccable programming. He did the same with music. He took us to the source of music, showed us where it came from, how to translate it to a story, a theme, a dialog, a punctuation. He taught us how to understand it from the source, not from the notes on paper. He did same with language, mysticism, business, dancing, writing, sports, dressing and living. He always encouraged us to point our beaks toward the sky, to reach for the highest ideal in all of our endeavors, whatever they may be. He taught us through the Highest Yoga Tantra.

Rama used his power to transmute our consciousness, to make us clearer perceivers, more conscious, more awake. But, he said, it was the responsibility of the student to learn and master the material. Rama used to ask, "Which is better, to teach someone how to make a million dollars or to give them a million dollars? If you give it to them, once they spend it, it is gone. If you teach them how to make it, they will always have that knowledge. No one will ever be able to take it away." He believed in teaching us *how*, and he created situations that inspired us to transform, to make jumps, to see past the surface to the heart of life. He gave us tasks, raised our awareness, and then shooed us out the door: "Go figure it out."

Over and over, he asked us to reach, to stretch to the next step. Each task we attempted, if we did it with an enthusiastic attitude and an open heart, pushed the envelope of our capability. As a teacher, he compelled us to expand our minds, our wills, our hearts, working out the endless stream of modern day koans that he gave us. Our adventures, though seemingly outer, were always fraught with inner roadblocks, obstacles to our Enlightenment. We had to face our prejudices, fears, laziness, jealousies, anger, attractions and aversions through real world experience. No stone went unturned. His light shined upon every aspect of our being, from the highest to the lowest. In the process, we learned that everything is inside of us; all horror, all beauty, and ultimately, he showed us how to go beyond it all, to the still center of being.

As long as we stuck with it, one roadblock after another disintegrated. Rama used to say, "Just keep coming. Just stick with it." After difficult experiences, we were always rewarded with a freer, more luminous self. The sheer terror of looking honestly into the depths of our beings cultivated an uncanny sense of humor, another authentic trademark of Rama and his teachings. We learned through the course of our study with Rama that the illusion of separation is what limits us. Rama didn't believe in learning through hearing words, he insisted on learning through personal experience.

The Highest Yoga Tantra

Rama was a warrior and a bodhisattva. His fast path to Enlightenment was challenging and exciting, and it was packed with moments of supreme ecstasy, brilliance and humor. There was constant discovery, renewal, dissolution, and transformation. Although Rama was eclectic in his teachings, he made Tantra our ideal, and meditation the essence of our practice. Tantra is a path that deals with the reconciliation of opposites. Rather than running away from the world, it encourages the student to deal with the world in a realistic way, to accept it, without getting caught up or hung up in it. It is the path to Enlightenment in one lifetime. In Tantra, the student goes beyond systems, doctrines and religions and dives into the center of things. Rama taught us to embrace life, yet to be still enough to experience Eternity at the core of all aspects of living. He taught us to seek or reject experience not on the basis of dogma or current moral standards, but rather on the basis of following the highest Dharma, or Truth. He always told us to do what is right.

Rama made Tantra relevant to his students in today's world, translating it for the modern day seeker. He taught us through the modality of our time, and fitted his teachings into the current structures of today. Whether it was business, technology, modern music, or chic dressing, Rama encouraged his students to take it on, and through embracing it, to learn focus, impeccability and style. He taught us how to become so one-pointed in our meditation practice, that no matter what activities we were engaged in, we learned to bring our highest self to the activity, and to experience the silence at the core of it. Rama took heat for this, but he was teaching us true Tantra. It is a traditional, though extremely intense method for attaining Enlightenment in one lifetime. Rama made the ancient methods appropriate to a modern, Western world. If one were to conduct even a bit of research, it would become quickly obvious that all truly Enlightened teachers throw out the stagnant rituals and dogmas of past traditions and make Enlightenment vital, alive and applicable to the current time. The ridicule that he got was not so unlike what Guatama Buddha, Padmasambhava and Ramakrishna had to endure to bring the same truth to seekers in their time.

In the twenty years that Rama worked with his students, he borrowed from numerous paths, but through it all, Tantra was our ideal and meditation was the essence of our practice. Aldous Huxley refers to the essential core, the indescribable fact of most religions as the "Perennial Philosophy in its chemically pure state", in his introduction to the *Bhagavad-Gita*. He states that it can only be known through contemplation, and that once it is set down in words, no matter how undogmatic they are, a bias is superimposed onto them. Rama guided us to that essential core, reminding us continually that it was all within us. Om Mani Padme Hum, the mantra of Avalokiteshvara – Enlightenment is Within. He didn't necessarily tell us what we wanted to hear, and he didn't give us pat answers. He showed us truth by his own example, by transmitting light and consciousness to us, and by weaving beautiful and complex mandalas into our beings that pointed us back to ourselves.

Tantra is called *the razor's edge* because with meditation and transformation comes the unleashing of power. As we became empowered, our desires were amplified. As focus was strengthened, we were able to point it in any direction, either toward our Enlightenment or toward the fulfillment of our desires. We learned the hard way, through our own undoing and at the expense of Rama's body, what it means to abuse power. We were forced to look at the imprinting and samskaras that have kept us from Enlightenment lifetime after lifetime. The door was always open to leave, and some people chose to bow out. Rama never spoke disparagingly about people who left, rather he wished them well on their continued spiritual journey. He always held his students in the highest regard. Those of us who stayed gave him license to pop our bubbles of illusion and egotism. And he used any means to do this, whether by making us laugh at ourselves, speaking the harsh truth to us, or inspiring us with Dharma talk in magnificent, even opulent settings.

The Path in Today's World

Rama used the modern day arena as the platform from which to teach his students. He did not avoid anything because it was of the world. The basic Tantric premise is that Nirvana is here, where we are right now, not in some far away land, some distant time, or some other world. In order to discover this, one must be able to stop thought, to meditate. Although living and working in the world is an extremely difficult path, it has faster, more powerful results. Renouncing the world and cloistering away, out of temptation's reach, denying those parts of life that could cause one to "sin", or waver from the path, is a viable tradition. On the Tantric path, however, the student aims to experience Nirvana, or the still center of being, in all situations, experiences and feelings. Rather than running away from money, for instance, the Tantric student sees it simply for what it is, an exchange vehicle. It is not money itself that corrupts. It is the intent behind it that matters. In the same way, sex is not inherently bad. It is the intent behind it that is either twisted or pure. Similarly with business, if the intent is to do excellent work, to stay mindful and to maintain integrity, then business can become an intrinsic part of the path. When viewing these prominent parts of daily living on the planet without a cultural or moral spin, and instead with unbiased, objective right understanding, the cultural stigma is deflated and they lose their emotional tension. Through inner stillness and detachment, the student of Tantra can use any aspect of living to gain deeper understanding, go beyond desire and ego, and gain self-mastery.

Rama created a program that combined career development, martial arts, literature, film, contemporary music, fashion, sports and travel. He used the components of our culture through which to teach and express higher consciousness.

Rama encouraged his students to enter the world of computer technology. First, it is a wonderful way to focus the mind. In the practice of Zen, there are two stances for meditation. The first is sitting in meditation and stopping thought (zazen), reaching sublime states of stillness, wonder and oneness. The result of this experience is insight, compassion and knowledge. The second meditative stance is mindfulness, in which the student keeps the mind focused and still throughout the course of daily activity. In this way, the mind is not left to wander aimlessly through daydreams or redundant, meaningless and chaotic thoughts. It is believed by the practitioner of meditation that maintaining a clear state of mind keeps the mind intuitive, agile and ready to learn.

In former times, Tibetan Buddhist monks were given complex geometrical images called mandalas to visualize and hold perfectly in their minds. This allowed them to stretch and strengthen their minds while practicing focus on detailed and complex visualizations, enabling them to reach to new levels of light, and new depths of understanding in their meditation practice. Computer programming can accomplish the same thing. It's possible for a person to strengthen their mind and improve their meditation if they focus on writing excellent programming code or designing a complex database system. Programming is a wonderful balance to sitting meditation, and can work as a simple gauge for maintaining clarity and equilibrium.

Programming also allows the student to be self-reliant. The computer industry is booming with far greater demand than supply, making it fairly easy to find high paying jobs. Since we live in a Judeo Christian society where Buddhism is not held in high regard, it is impractical to create the usual monastic situation that would have worked centuries ago. Instead of living in a monastery, Rama encouraged us to create our own sanctuaries within the confines of our homes. So, most of Rama's students are aesthetically oriented toward clean, quiet, beautiful surroundings that are conducive to meditation.

Business is also a dynamic platform from which to practice Tantra. The moves are quick, and one must be frosty to succeed. In business, the student learns to take energy, as in the martial arts Aikido and Judo, and use the opponent's energy to make interesting counter moves. It requires control and intuition. It is the perfect situation for the Tantric student that feels strong enough to try their hand. Even mistakes are taken as meaningful lessons that uncover glitches in the self, imperfections, desires, and ego. It is an interesting learning ground for people whose proclivities would normally move them in more solitary directions. It is a way to expand mind, and with one's back against the wall in real world scenarios, it is a sure way to develop will and intellect, both of which are necessary to reach and maintain higher states of consciousness.

Rama was an athlete, a black belt and martial arts teacher, a certified technical scuba diver (he dove to depths of 300 feet), and a certified dive master. He was always sure to tune his students in to the latest and greatest involving martial arts, diving and snowboarding. Many of Rama's students have black belts in one or several martial arts. In addition to other benefits, the study of martial arts helped Rama's students understand the etiquette of the student-teacher relationship. Sports such as snowboarding and diving are great ways to enjoy nature, have fun, and increase kundalini energy, which is the essential energy of progress, life, and meditation.

The History

Rama (pre-1980)

Rama was born on February 9, 1950 in San Diego, California, and grew up in Stamford, Connecticut. He became interested in Buddhist teachings when he was twelve. After leaving high school, he traveled extensively and came to learn about meditation and Self-Realization. It became a way of life for him. He started teaching shortly thereafter, and wrote several books that allowed him to tour and interview. He also obtained his Ph.D. in English Literature from the State University of New York at Stonybrook, where he graduated summa cum laude.

He began to gather a small group of students with whom he worked closely, and who were his good friends. In 1979, he moved with them out to San Diego, trusting that the Infinite would work things out. Together the small band found a beautiful house with an expansive view of the Pacific, and Rama started his California teaching adventures.

During the course of 1980, small numbers of students came, and Rama opened up his home as the Anahata Center. The living room was clean, somewhat simple, and warm for social conversation. The two main rooms of the house were cleared for holding meditation classes. The powder blue carpet was thick and cushiony, and Rama held many meetings with his students and with visitors. The kitchen was open to the far room, and many feasts were prepared by Rama for his students.

As the year went on, Rama continued progressing in his meditations. He had gone into samadhi intermittently through the years, and was starting to cycle up through the lofty ranges of illumination more and more frequently. By the end of that year, Rama was going into samadhi day after day, night after night. The gold light rolled off of him in concentric circles. Everyone who came into contact with him at this time became enveloped in the ecstasy. Rama, at 30, was breaking through the first stages of his Enlightenment. During the course of this process, he saw that Eternity was now his teacher, and he broke ties with his former guru. Once he cut that cord, he cycled up so fast, no one, including him, was primed for what happened next.

The Ramakrishna Years (1980 – 1983)

Rama continued to cycle up, his meditations becoming more powerful, his samadhi experiences becoming more grounded in his everyday life. People flocked to him. Being in his auric range had a transformative effect. A person immediately experienced heightened awareness in his presence. All who came were bathed in light. The gold hues that emanated from his body were visceral. He gave high Dharma talks that inspired students and visitors, igniting the fire of knowledge and aspiration within each. He gave all the moments of his life to extending his light to others; he taught ceaselessly. He embodied Karma Yoga, the path of selfless giving, caring more about the welfare of others than himself. Everything he did caused him to continue cycling upwards.

Sitting in meditation with Rama, one could see beyond the chains of the human condition. We easily and smoothly broke through the inner barriers and limitations that confined us and boxed us into a fixed set of ideas about life and ourselves. We saw miraculous sights, experienced extraordinary states of sublime and luminous awareness. We all had a sense that we were beholding a rare phenomenon, yet we had no point of reference. We rode his energy as we sailed through the portals of higher consciousness, over the endless oceans of Eternity.

Rama, who had been an intense and one-pointed seeker up to this time, had always been fairly serious, though he had a proclivity toward humor. Once his samadhis started overtaking him, one tsunami wave after another, all baggage that was not supportive to his Enlightenment process was dropped. The inner revolution that he experienced was the kind of revolution that comes from the core of existence. This kind of revolution is the greatest fear and threat to the human condition, and thus to mainstream society and mainstream religion. Rama gave himself over as a pure and willing instrument of the Dharma. He became spontaneous, compassionate and outrageously funny.

Though Rama was swept day after day into the rushing river of Dharma, his inner surrender was balanced by a conservative and very grounded outer life. In Carlos Castaneda's books, it is what Don Juan refers to as *controlled folly*. Similarly, when one learns to master the piano through hard work and daily exercises, the ability to be creative and improvise, that is, to play the piano with abandon, becomes more and more possible. So too, Rama continued to tighten his life. He exercised daily, his finances were in order, his house was impeccable, and all aspects of his life were in perfect balance. He brought focus and one-pointedness to his daily activities as well as to his students and to his Enlightenment process.

During this time, there was incredible excitement in all of our lives. He allowed us to sail the inner skies with him. He opened up the doors to all that wanted in. As his awareness continued to cycle up, he started to attain siddha powers. These are powers that come with intensive meditation and stopping thought for prolonged periods of time. They are perceived from the mundane awareness as miracles, but are actually the manipulation of energy and light in the subtle realms that ripple into the physical realm. Those who were able to still their minds and silence their thoughts saw many of Rama's feats. During meditation talks and seminars, he used his siddha powers to transmute consciousness from the mundane to the supraconscious. During excursions to places of power such as the desert or ocean, he used the powers to lift his students into higher states of awareness, where they could see and experience existence in ways that they could not on their own.

In our day and time, there is an incredible planetary cynicism that has strangled the ability to have faith in that which goes beyond logic. Yet, the phenomenon of siddha powers has been occurring on the planet for thousands of years. Should the reader want a cross check of this extraordinary circumstance placed in a historical context, simply pick up any book of Tibetan Yoga, Tantric Yoga, Hindu Yoga, or Buddhism, and you will find that this is a standard aspect of paths leading to Enlightenment (e.g. *Tibetan Book of Great Liberation*, Evans-Wentz, 1954).

As Rama continued his journey, he became more and more absorbed in higher consciousness. He taught Dharma to anyone who wanted to receive it. Every time we sat with him, he went into ecstatic reverie. More students came and Rama's responsibilities increased. People wanted Rama to take responsibility for their inner progress. During these first years, he was extremely open. He couldn't say no to anyone. As he became more empowered, so did his students. He made many efforts to teach us how to use this power constructively. People who gain tremendous power, without having developed purity, humility and self-control tend to abuse it and can harm themselves or others.

The Zen Master Emerges (1983 – 1985)

As Rama's mission became clearer to him, he donned the attitude of a warrior in order to accomplish his Dharmic tasks. He knew that it would take a high degree of intensity to withstand the rigors of bringing Dharma to this violent and chaotic planet. For him to continue cycling upwards while continuing to work with his students and the world meant making some changes in his life. Intensive and potent energies were coming at him, both from the world and from his students.

Rama's mission took him to other cities, where he gave public lectures. He started to become more discriminating in accepting students. He became more detached from the students who were close to him so that he could devote more time to administering a clean, Western-oriented environment for his many new students to learn and grow in. He became more concerned for the welfare of the many, and less concerned for his private friendships.

Rama was giving everything he had. The structures of our inner and outer lives dissolved and reformed over and over. At the end of 1983, Rama changed his program and asked half of his eight hundred students to leave. Though this was personally a difficult decision for him, he was acting as an instrument of the Dharma, and saw that this was the proper thing to do.

Rama emphasized computer science as a career path, and many of his students at this time began developing their careers in earnest. Rama knew that hard work and a disciplined life would aid us in our self-discovery in many ways, including providing us with self-reliance and economic independence. Rama taught us that we could gauge our successful usage and application of energy by our progress in career development.

Career Development and Transformation (1985 – 1990)

Rama's Enlightenment process was continually accelerating. He no longer looked like the same man we met several years before. He was more chiseled, his skin more translucent, his power level far beyond any range that we could recognize or achieve. Rama charged tuition fees for his instruction, leading seminars in a Western university-like program.

Once a student was on-board with the program, life became extremely exciting. The challenge was to become more successful at stopping thought and translating the energy gained to a progressive life. Rama continued giving seminars across the country, and those who came signed up for the full program, including meditation and computer science. Once we got the basics down, Rama started to give us more difficult tasks including new programming languages, new database expertise, and new business industries. The path was about transformation, making jumps, moving ahead and expanding our minds. Rama advocated hard work. If we took on the challenge, becoming an ace software consultant was inevitable. We were a manager's dream because career was our path, and we strove for excellence.

Rama raised the bar by increasing our tuition as we progressed, knowing for us worldly success was tied to spiritual progress. He kept us from wasting this most auspicious lifetime, by nudging and cajoling us into further transformation, when we could have reveled in our seeming successes, stopping short of Enlightenment. He was providing us with classes, and with each new class, with each new task, we improved our career profiles. Each of these jumps was indicative of correct and successful application of the energy, and provided a doorway to another level of consciousness or a door for people to leave. Of course, there were some who left in a sour grapes mode, but most people who left the program were grateful for what they had learned, and continued to practice what Rama had taught them. With our increased economic success, we were able to develop meditative sanctuaries, take trips to places of power, and through our tuition, contribute to Rama's Dharma projects.

We started new businesses, developed teaching software for kids, developed animated software of spiritual books and systems, and saw Rama intermittently as he continued transmuting our consciousness. In 1985, Rama also began composing music and working with three of his musician students in a group that he named Nirvana. He later changed the name of the group to Zazen, and he often played Zazen's albums or most recent work at our meetings. Rama was also the producer of all of the Zazen albums.

Rama continued being ruthlessly honest, exposing our illusions to us, always with humor, love and compassion. Sometimes his students became angry and confused – it is not easy to face the darker aspects of our selves. He took the anger and frustration and continued to progress his students on their pathway to Enlightenment, although this took a heavy toll on his health. Many Enlightened teachers through time have chosen to transmute their students' karmas through their own bodies, in an act of pure sacrifice and love. This gives the student a real chance at becoming Enlightened in one lifetime. Rama was one of these rare teachers, though his students' ability to comprehend his giving was fairly limited.

Teaching and Business (1990 – 1995)

Rama was soaring, imbued with power, yet his compassion deepened, and his commitment to his students continued to be unfaltering. Times were getting darker, and his students were becoming confused in the midst of the world's chaos and from the pull of their own samskaras. Ups and downs were getting more extreme. So Rama gave his students the task of teaching in order to provide a counterbalance. We taught meditation in various cities throughout the country and in Europe. We gave lectures where we taught people meditation techniques and the ancient precepts of generating energy, focus, success and compassion. During this time, many of Rama's students began to understand the intensity and commitment involved in teaching correctly. We saw the pain of humanity in a new way. We began to feel compassion, and to realize that our self-absorption was limiting and painful. We began to realize the giving, joy and beauty that come with ushering another seeker into higher awareness. We became more committed to our own practice.

In the mid-90's, Rama stepped up his computer science program once again to teach his newest students how to successfully apply the energy generated in meditation to career and living. The older students continued advancing their careers in business. Rama started many new business, music and software ventures during this time, using business as an advanced platform from which to conduct his enlightened dialogs with his students, similar to Krishna on the battlefield with Arjuna in the *Bhagavad-Gita*.

CONCLUSION

At present, Rama's students are the results of his labor. There are approximately equal numbers of men and women. The men and women who learned Rama's teachings are some of the most successful in their chosen fields of endeavor. Throughout Rama's teaching, he empowered women to traverse the rugged terrains of higher consciousness and liberation. It was one of the key focal points of his life. Rama taught women students to go beyond their conditioning, to become full human beings outside of role constraints, and to reach their highest potential, in spite of all obstacles faced by women in our society.

Rama's students enjoy leading exciting lives, in the tradition of Rama himself. Rama nurtured a celebratory joy of life, and like him, we love to travel, snowboard, dive, hike and practice martial arts. Many also create and play music. We are continually upgrading our technological and business skills through ongoing education, and in general, we are an extremely funny bunch of people.

Rama showed us, through his life, the beauty and reality of Enlightenment. He treated all those he met with equanimity and compassion. He donned the attitude of a supreme warrior, though he kept himself open and vulnerable to Eternity. He taught us how to dive deeply within, to the eternal nature of our beings.

He created a complex, multifaceted, infinite mandala within each one of us. He wove his Enlightenment and his love into us all. He packed us with symbols, and created doorways to perfect knowledge and to the unfolding of infinite discoveries. All we have to do is be silent, listen, and reach.

Our gratitude to Rama is immeasurable.

The morning in the desert,
The autumn afternoon,
The sky as the sun sets,
The wind blowing –
There are only moments.

There is only Enlightenment,
All the rest is illusion.
In the beginning, in the end,
There is only light.

There is no beginning, there is no end,
There are only moments.
Victory, defeat, despair – are only moments.
None are final, none are conclusive.

The important moments are these moments,
The moments you are alive.
You learn that what matters is not you,
But living beyond yourself.

My happiness comes from doing all I can for my students.
To help them, what else could there be?
To see them succeed, to see them improve,
That is what matters.

-     Rama
August 1, 1994

Teaching

In 1992, Rama took his students on a trip to the Big Island of Hawaii. On one sunny afternoon, I was alone by a fishpond reading a book. Suddenly, I heard a strange splashing noise coming from the pond. It didn't stop, and I wondered if an animal had fallen in to the pond and couldn't get out. When I came closer to investigate, I saw that it was a little fish swimming back and forth across the surface of the pond. It was so close to the surface that its head actually stuck out of the water and its fins caused the noisy splashing that I was hearing. I thought it was bizarre, because I had grown up in Hawaii and had seen a lot of fishponds, and I had never seen a fish acting like this. It seemed so agitated, but there was no danger or any threat that I could see. In fact, all the other fish were hanging out quietly near the bottom of the pond acting completely normal.

The fish was still splashing back and forth when Rama strode up to the edge of the pond and stood watching its antics for a few moments with an amused air. I said, "He's been doing that for about half an hour already. It's so weird!" Smiling, he turned to me and exclaimed, "That's my kind of fish!" I wasn't sure what he meant so I just waited for him to continue. After watching the fish for a few moments longer, he walked over to me and explained that the fish was "trying to get somewhere the other fish weren't." He said, "You see, *that's* what it takes to become Enlightened! You have to do things other people don't, and you have to do it with utter determination and complete abandon, just like that fish. To everyone else it might look crazy, but if it's important to you, who cares? You do it anyway; you do it because you have to, because you're fed up with the normal fields of perception and want to get someplace better, someplace that is more interesting for *you*. These other fish aren't going there, they don't care – but to him it matters, and that's why he swims like that!"

Then he asked me if I had read the Buddhist Bible we had in our hotel rooms, which he had recommended that we all read (since there are a large number of Japanese tourists in Hawaii, most major hotels keep both Christian and Buddhist Bibles in the guest rooms). I had read a little but had given up because it was very metaphorical and relied on imagery that I mostly didn't understand. But I told him about one part I had read that described a sword plunging into the earth and coming out with seven different things attached to it. The last thing was a dragon, and the text said to "throw away all, but save the dragon." I didn't have any idea what that meant, but Rama explained it to me. He said, "The dragon is Enlightenment. The rest of the things that are pulled up with the dragon represent the clutter in your life, the things and the people that complicate it and drag you down. It's saying you should get rid of everything else and focus *only* on Enlightenment, if that is what you seek."

Rama's comments radically altered my perception of what it means to be a spiritual seeker. I had never considered people who were interested in self-discovery or self-realization to be particularly brave or strong. In fact, I thought it was usually the opposite case, that people drawn to self-discovery were sensitive but rather weak and they tended to be easily overwhelmed or overrun by the rest of the world. That was how I saw myself. But this encounter with Rama, a true teacher of Enlightenment and self-discovery, showed me that the process actually takes tremendous courage, dedication, willpower and a lot of heart! I saw that it wasn't about running away from life; in fact, it was the opposite. Studying with a spiritual teacher suddenly didn't seem so different than training for the Olympics or managing a serious career, because I understood that it takes a similar one-pointed concentration and extreme determination to "succeed" in spite of all the obstacles.

The other thing I came to understand and appreciate on this trip was the amazing capacity Rama had to turn the smallest, silliest detail of a moment into a lesson about life and Enlightenment!

Driving south from Los Angeles, the sign for the La Jolla off ramp appears almost two hours before Rama's living-room lecture is set to start. To pass the time, I decide to visit Torrey Pines Reserve, approximately ten miles north of La Jolla in the beach town of Del Mar.

Bypassing Del Mar's tourist gauntlet/main-street, I exit, make a quick left onto the Pacific Coast Highway and drive up a steep hill running south from a long, curving stretch of white sand.

Torrey Pines Reserve is one of nature's anomalies — an outcropping of huge boulders, sandstone cliffs and rare, centuries-old, pine trees. The pines furthest from the beach, sheltered from the pummeling wind, grow hundreds of feet tall. A park information brochure states that the cliffs are among the oldest geological formations in southern California, that their wrinkled, reddish surfaces have yielded archaeological discoveries dating back millions of years; that the small valleys and secluded alcoves are home to one-of-a-kind species of plants and wildlife.

I park near a grassy mesa and notice twenty or more well-dressed people bunched together on a windswept knoll overlooking the sea. Among them is a bride in a long white dress and streaming veil, her black-suited mate by her side, merged modestly into the multitude of guests. Even from a distance, the bride looks exultant, radiant.

Twenty yards from my car, I spot a pathway crossing the mesa. The path soon leads where no wedding parties are likely to be - down a narrow, twisting gully that plunges steeply into the trees and shrubbery. After less than ten minutes of trekking — careful placement of smooth-soled street shoes on slippery sandstone — I'm surrounded by red cliffs and towering pines. In the distance, waves crash rhythmically to shore.

The scent of the pines, the late afternoon sun bursting in brilliant patches of light among the interwoven branches, the shapes of sturdy pines casting long shadows along the path — all these beckon me forward. Pine needles mass in fragrant heaps on the ground; black ants and green beetles circle busily over them.

As I walk further downhill, the foliage becomes denser, the air cooler. Peering through the trees, I see the deeply etched carvings of the cliffs appear in dramatic, varied tableaus.

This exotic locale, so unexpected amidst a shoreline of elegant beach homes and manicured racetracks, has so absorbed me that I avoid taking notice of a hiker moving rapidly up the path. I turn my head to exclude the oncoming hiker from even the edge of my vision so I can focus uninterruptedly on the surrounding beauty. Only when the person is several feet directly in front of me, and one of us must step aside to make room, do I raise my eyes.

I stare without blinking at what I see — a tall man, sporting a rather worn orange tee shirt, dusty hiking boots, faded green shorts and a bemused smile.

It's Rama.

I feel like a tornado lifts me off my feet and sets me down again.

"What are you doing here?" I yelp, as if Rama had no right to occupy a park trail at the same time as me.

"I come here a lot," he answers calmly. "I like to meditate here." I look at him speechlessly, afraid he'll slip by.

"Can I ask you something?" My question is a stall.

"Sure," Rama says. "What's the question?" He shifts his weight and crosses his arms, as if he expects he might have to stay a few minutes longer than expected. But the crisp tone of his voice discourages additional bluffing. I watch his hair blow reddish gold into the wind. My questions are: 1) How come you can make me feel weightless? 2) Why am I earthbound when you seem aerial? 3) How do I get to be like you?

"How much longer do you think you'll be holding lectures at your house, Rama?" I say.

"I've just been thinking about that," he answers. Bingo.

Rama motions for me to follow him, and we walk several yards off the trail to a large, flat boulder with a birds-eye view of treetops and a distant expanse of turquoise-green sea. We sit on the rock, several feet apart, facing the water. The heat of the stone feels soothing as it warms the back of my legs and spreads upward, relaxing my entire body.

"That was a good question," Rama says, once I'm settled. "You see, when I moved here from the East Coast about a year-and-a-half ago, I'd already been teaching meditation for ten years. I wasn't sure what the response would be. It's been great."

I nod my head in agreement.

"I'm going to end the talks at my house this month because there's no space for all the people," he continues. "There are so many students driving from Los Angeles that I plan to start holding seminars in L.A., and soon I'll start giving them in San Francisco." His tone is so matter-of-fact that I can't tell if he's pleased or not.

"That's good news, right?"

"Yes," Rama says gently, looking at the point where the ocean and horizon meet. "But it means things will change. Up 'til now, we've been kind of a small group. Laughing a lot.

4

Helping each other. If someone needed a car, we chipped in and bought it for them. If someone wanted to go back to school, I found a way to pay for their enrollment. When there's only twenty or thirty people in a room, you get to know everyone well. When there's several hundred people in a room, you know them well - I feel every one of their pains and desires acutely -but you don't sit with them and have conversations like this."

Rama looks at me briefly, a piercing sidelong glance. He has given me new information. I can imagine myself sitting in front of a lot of people and pontificating philosophical truths. I can imagine absorbing their admiration. But I can't imagine willingly absorbing other people's pains, desires and frustrations. I'm struck by the thought that Rama feels my pains and desires. Multiplying my discomfort by hundreds to thousands of people is frightening. I suddenly understand the sensation I feel when I look in Rama's eyes —the endlessness, not only of awareness, but also of human suffering and its antidote, compassion.

"There's not much of a choice, is there?" I say.

"There's always a choice," Rama responds. "At any moment you're free to make decisions which increase your own happiness or increase the happiness of others. I've found that increasing the happiness of others makes me happy. That's the Buddhist way. You give beyond the point of exhaustion. When you think you have nothing left to give, you give more. That's my choice. It's not for everyone."

A large red and black bird alights on the branch of the pine tree closest to our light-dappled boulder. A red-winged blackbird with a taut, powerful wing span, it throws its head back and looks eagerly into the sky. The sun, low in the horizon, casts long shadows behind Rama and me, extending the shadow of our bodies through the trees and branches, across the jagged cliffs. The blackbird preens and hops from twig to twig.

Rama also observes the bird's antics as it explores its temporary perch.

"You need to learn from everything around you," he says, and I realize he's referring to himself as well as to me. "Wisdom is learning to be like that bird. To love life deeply — the textures, the scents, the sea, the city. To love life wherever circumstances might take you."

With a staccato dip of its beak, the bird scoops up a pine needle, spreads its wings and takes flight to the north, vanishing from sight.

"I love life now," I tell Rama, "But if you'd asked me two hours ago, I would have said that life sucks. Big time." I tell Rama what happened in my tour of duty as publicist for a famous television personality, how sad and uncomfortable I felt around her.

"I think you're being too judgmental," he comments, when I've finished listing her flaws. "She's achieved a type of wisdom most people would be very happy for." I look at him quizzically.

"There's a wisdom in leading a successful life, in being sharp, clear and focused in achieving your goals," he says. "[She] achieved a form of worldly wisdom that offers lessons you can learn. But there's another aspect of wisdom, which you and I are interested in. We respect someone who's successful in life, but at the same time we know there's more — that wisdom is allowing yourself to be still, to reflect, to be conscious.

"We know that achieving only worldly success will never lead to happiness. That's the first point the Buddha taught. The Four Noble Truths — do you know them?"

I can feel my skin turning red. I hate that feeling because my freckles stand out. With embarrassment, I admit that I don't exactly know what the Buddha's Four Noble Truths are. I've heard of them - I think they're like what the Ten Commandments are to the Jews or the Sermon on the Mount is to Christians. But I couldn't list them. I look silently at Rama and shake my head.

"I'll tell you," he says. "The abridged version.

> "One, the life of an unenlightened person is filled with suffering."

> "Two, the cause of suffering is a lack of Enlightenment, which is caused by a person's attachment to desires and aversion to suffering.

> "Three, there's a way to reach Enlightenment and get beyond suffering.

> "Four, meditation is the pathway to Enlightenment."

Rama looks at me, his eyes twinkling. "Now you know it all," he says. I smile broadly.

"Of course," he adds, looking again towards the sea, "the Buddha spent his life teaching and elaborating upon those four main truths. Just as you will spend your life seeking to understand them in deeper and more personal ways.

"I think your complaint with [her] is that she's trapped in point one — attachment to desire and fear of suffering. But that's no reason to judge her. Life is cyclical. Many people who embrace a spiritual life first explore the material world, if only to find out how devoid it is of lasting happiness. The Buddha himself was a prince who led an inconceivable — by today's standards — life of wealth, power and sensual pleasure. He gave up that life after he saw human suffering for the first time, and vowed to find a way to overcome suffering."

In the silence that follows, a patch of piercing orange sunlight illuminates a wrinkled corner of the rock. I feel so palpably still that I sense I can rise into silence, raise powerful wings to soar in silence, become it. I feel I am more silence than person.

"It's interesting," Rama says as an afterthought, his voice lifting me like an updraft. "In the Far East, the wise are thought of as followers; in the West, as leaders."

His words remind me of *The Way of Life* – a compilation of sayings by Lao Tzu, a Chinese philosopher who lived around 600 B.C. and whose teachings became the basis of Taoism. I recall some of my favorite passages, memorized with gender switches:

> The sanest woman
> Sets up no deed,
> Lays down no law,
> Takes everything that happens as it comes,
> As something to animate, not appropriate,
> To earn, not to own,
> To accept naturally without self-importance:
> If you never assume importance
> You never lose it.

Or

> She who feels punctured
> Must once have been a bubble…
> A woman with insight
> Knows that to keep under is to endure.

Side by side, Rama and I gaze at the horizon as winglike patterns spread endlessly across the surface of the sea. A smooth, free-of-thought power spreads through me in expansive patterns. My surroundings appear perfectly flat, as if painted on a two-dimensional surface.

7

No one walks by to disturb our peace, as primordial as breath.

Then the blackbird streaks back into view, alighting with red and black ceremony on the tree directly in front of us. With each brisk movement of the bird's head and beak, claws wrapped tightly around a sturdy branch, the world returns to three-dimensional fullness.

"I love that bird," I tell Rama, and at that moment I do love it, wholeheartedly, for being small with attitude.

Rama smiles.

"There are templates in life that will guide you," Rama remarks softly. "There are templates in the universe you can follow. To see them you must make your mind quiet and still. And you must be happy with your life. If your mind is restless, if you're unhappy emotionally, if you can't settle down, you can't see anything but your own restlessness and confusion."

The blackbird hops onto a slim branch. Under the bird's weight, the branch drops perilously towards the ground. The bird maintains its grip, undisturbed by its rapid vertical swing.

"Wisdom is knowing that if you bend, you don't have to break," Rama laughs.

I smile at the blackbird's timing. "I understand life offers templates," I say. "I know life is a great teacher. But isn't it wise - when you've found a teacher - to spend as much time with that teacher as possible?"

"Not necessarily," Rama replies strongly. He leans forward, folds his hands over his knees and looks at me earnestly.

"The etiquette of interacting with a teacher is something you'll learn over time. There are no role models in the West. It's important to understand that you don't have to be physically present with a teacher in order to learn from or receive empowerment from your teacher."

I look at him skeptically. I think he's trying to brush me off gracefully,

"No bull," he says matter-of-factly. "All you have to do to be in touch with your teacher is to think of them with positivity, respect and enthusiasm for their work and teachings. If you can't do that, you won't be very connected with them, but then again, why would you want to be if you don't feel those feelings?"

Rama looks towards the distant water.

"You don't have to sit on a rock with me," he says in a soft tone. "It's not necessary for the sea to turn lavender in the sunset. The sky above us doesn't need to explode with coral clouds."

He pauses. "We're always sitting on this rock, don't you see? When you want to find me, come here in your mind, or go to the desert with me, or sit in my house in La Jolla. Those moments don't go away. When you think of them, you'll be there."

Rama shakes his head slightly. "I don't believe it's necessary — or even desirable — for a student to try to spend too much time with their teacher. If the student likes what the teacher is saying, they should take those teachings and put them into practice in their own life. As a Buddhist teacher, I emphasize meditation and mindfulness. And I offer ways you can empower your life — basically in order to increase your ability to meditate and be mindful. And if, in your mindfulness, you choose to establish an inner connection with your teacher, then you should do so."

I look around - at the deepening shadows, the purple sea, the pale orange clouds tinged with gold spreading across the horizon, the full, deep-green boughs of the Torrey pines. I hear not one bird but many, a chorus of birdsong, and in the distance, the raucous caws of seagulls. Three feet from me is Rama, his eyes now closed, deep in meditation. I nod my head. I understand.

Many times during his years of teaching, Rama talked to his students about very advanced Tantric Buddhist topics such as "inverses", "folding space" and "karmic recoding".

Although I generally accepted that he performed these complex, highly sophisticated transformative processes for us (because the results immediately became obvious), the majority of the time I did not see the actual mechanics of the process. His mastery of the karmic transformation process of his students was so refined, so smooth, and seemingly effortless, that it was difficult to see the brilliance of the work being performed.

Rama was a true Master. He was a multidimensional, multi-lifetime cosmic Cray supercomputer, who was an expert in the compositional coding of beings, the structural patterns and causal weaves which compose a soul. The closest he came to comparing it to anything of this physical world was likening it to genetic coding and playing with the RNA/DNA of a physical being. However, Rama worked in other realms with the karmic coding which bound a soul to particular formations and controlled its destiny. He was so powerful with this skill that when he manipulated a student's karmic coding, his or her destiny was shifted forever, and often the memory of having been any other way was totally erased. What a gift for souls interested in the short path to Enlightenment! Rama explained that he simply "folded space".

The one time that Rama permitted us to actually witness this powerful process occurred in late 1988. Before he began, he told us he was going to permit us to see into his diamond mind, to actually watch his processes while he "folded space" for us.

He began the demonstration with a "basic structural inversion". As my mind melded with his Enlightened mind, I saw myself in another dimension or universe affixed to the spinning Wheel of the Dharma. The transaction was extremely real. I spun around and around.

Then Rama amped up the energy, revealing a more "complex inversion". He did this several times. Each time that he upped the energy level, I saw a more powerful and infinitely more complex karmic manipulation. All of my future lifetimes were being changed forever in a very brilliant direction. And I saw that these gifts from Rama could never be undone or taken away.

By the last inversion, I saw a flattening of all of the curvatures of infinite space, literally a folding over of dimensions, one over another, and an incredible dance of bright geometric formations that shifted back and forth, split and united, whirled and stopped cold. And within all of this play of energy within Rama's Enlightened mind, I saw myself flattened, rounded, folded over, split and united, disassembled and reassembled, whirled and killed and revived into an immortal luminous being.

Rama told his students this story a couple of times, about the relationship between students and their teacher, and about learning how to find and stay "on the path".

Rama said a teacher always tells his or her students right up front, "Part of the job of the teacher is to tell you where the path is and where it is not. You might find this annoying, but what can we do? It's part of the teacher's job description. So, this is the path, and you want to stay on it. If you get off the path, you will find problems. Over there on your right is mud, and you don't want to go there because it will mess you up."

Of course, Rama said, the new student pays the teacher no mind and wanders off to find out what mud is about. "You go off and find out, yuck, this mud stuff isn't any good, and so you hustle back to the path and hope that no one has noticed." He laughed. We gathered that teachers always knew, whether they let on to it or not.

"Meanwhile," he said, "the teacher points out time and again that you don't want to go over there, or there or there. But over and over, the students will wander into these areas until they finally realize that they really don't like having to maneuver through brambles and quicksand and all the other things the teacher has been trying to warn them about.

"The teacher knows that if you are any good as a student, you will go off and have these experiences. Through ignoring and then discovering the correctness of what the teacher has said, the student learns to appreciate how much quicker and easier it is to do what is recommended rather than what is not. You have to learn this for yourself," Rama said, "through experience. Experience is what teaches you to trust your teacher, and to learn how and why to follow the path yourself."

Rama then went on to say, "There's a point when the path runs into water. It gets trickier there, because now the teacher has to point first to one rock and then another and tell you exactly where to step so you can continue and not hurt yourself. But because of the trust and understanding that has built up so far - because of when you went off the path as well as when you were on it - you take that first step out into the water. Well, some people don't, actually. They have hit their limit and they go away.

"For the people who are willing and who are ready, they take first the one step and then the next. And then," Rama said, "there comes the point where you can't actually see the rocks that the teacher is pointing to as you walk through the water. But again, you place your feet where the teacher has said, even though you can't see the rock yourself."

"Finally," Rama said, "there comes a time when the teacher is no longer there. They can't be. You have to cross the rest of the river yourself. But by then, you have learned how to do it for yourself. First you put one foot out and find a rock, and then the next."

Rama's students are now at that point. We are in the middle of the stream and there is no turning back. All we need to remember is that the path is taken, one careful step at a time, just as before. We have been fully prepared for this moment. We have been brought to this point with the full intention and love of an excellent teacher who knew exactly what he was doing, and who has displayed his trust that we will use every piece of what he has shared with us to succeed in crossing to the other side.

Rama once told me that I would never be as powerful as he was simply because I didn't love as much as he did.

Rama was a very versatile teacher and spoke to us about a wide range of topics. In particular, he taught us about meditation, martial arts and career success. No matter what the subject, however, there were always two underlying principles to everything Rama taught us. First and foremost, Rama always said, "What you focus on you become," and he encouraged us to always focus on Enlightenment and the brightest and happiest things in life. He also taught us that a basic thread through all of Tantric Buddhist teaching is to turn adversity into the pathway to Enlightenment. In the trial and tribulations of the modern world, we are fortunate to have plenty of opportunities to practice these ideals.

During an especially difficult period in my life, where it seemed that anything that could go wrong did go wrong, I turned to Rama as my last resort and remained completely focused on him, not knowing what else to do. Rather than getting angry or feeling sorry for myself, which would have been my typical response, for the first time, every new obstacle caused me to turn more and more to Rama. Each time I resorted to Rama, any negativity that I felt was dissipated, and I was left with a sense of humor about life. I realized that it was all just very funny! My situation hadn't changed, but my perceptions and my reactions had. Eventually, I came to a place of detachment from the physical events of my life and found that I was really happy and closer to Rama than I had ever been. Months later, Rama told me that I had handled that time in my life well. I was surprised to hear that he even knew what I had been going through, much less that he was happy about how I had applied his teachings. I came to understand what his wisdom meant to my life in a very practical way.

Rama told us a story about an incident that made an impression on him when he lived in Malibu. He was renting a house at the time, and one afternoon he could not find his dog. This was not that surprising, he said, because his dog was very social.

He went next door, found his dog, and had a chat with the woman who lived there. She was an elderly heiress, and she told Rama that she was learning to play the piano. Rama said he wondered for a moment why she would bother, since it seemed obvious to him that she "had one foot in the grave."

He thought about it afterward, and concluded that the woman had the right attitude. He said that she knew she wouldn't live long enough to be an excellent piano player, but she was nevertheless enthusiastic about life and about learning something new. He told us that this is a secret of living – to find new things to be enthusiastic about. Living with that attitude had kept her young, he said, and he urged us to be like that woman with our lives, to find new and interesting things to explore, always.

When Rama meditated with us, he often appeared to change into many different people. A few times, he looked like a lion, or a dragon. At the time of seeing these transformations they didn't seem strange because I wasn't thinking - I was just being there, experiencing. The first few times I did look away for a minute or blink my eyes to see if my vision was failing, but the perceptions always persisted. He would just morph from form to form.

Once, he changed into me! This time I did blink my eyes, even look away; I was sure I couldn't be seeing what I saw. But there it still was - framed in a circle of light, where Rama had been sitting, I saw myself. It made me quite uncomfortable. Then I had an insight - I was putting him on a pedestal in my mind, thinking of him as someone who was different from myself. Rama seemed to be telling me, psychically, that what he had attained, I could also.

Rama once told us a story. He was driving on a highway with one of his students. She was into ecology - saving the planet, recycling, the ozone layer - all that. She, along with most of the people on this planet, had some deep-seated, preconceived notions about Enlightenment based upon her ideas of "right" and "wrong". Rama wanted her to understand what Enlightenment is and is not. He was drinking a can of Coke, and when he finished, he rolled down his window and threw out the can. As he described the shocked, horrified look on her face, a mischievous smile stole across his own. He was illustrating a point. Enlightenment is not that. It's not about being a good person. It's not about Religion. Rama said, "Enlightenment is off the game board, folks."

A prime-time tabloid television program aired an entire show about Rama. Camera crews from the show filmed Rama teaching one of our computer classes, composing music with one of his students, and scuba diving in the Caribbean. They filmed a martial arts segment with Rama's students who were black belts. They also came to Rama's home to interview him. Later, Rama told us that the interview went for six hours straight, with no break.

Rama had told us before he was interviewed for the show that the program would be a slam against him and his work with us. He told us that even though it would be damaging to him personally, the show would be a way for people to learn about his book, *Surfing the Himalayas*, so he had agreed to participate.

When the show aired, some of us watched it together. At times we laughed at how ludicrous it was, but at other times we were angered by the way the press was treating someone who had spent his life trying to help others. Even though Rama had warned us about what they were going to do, we were still shocked at how he was mistreated.

Knowing we were upset, Rama met with all of us to talk about it. He posed the question to us: "What should we do in response?" Thoughts were whizzing around the room. Rama asked us if we should sue them. Initially, I thought that was a great idea. I was angry and wanted revenge. But Rama went on to talk about the amount of time we would have to spend in a courthouse. Obviously, we would win, but did we want to waste the next few years in a court battle? Didn't we have better things to do?

So what was the answer? Sensing the anger in the room, Rama made a brief mention of the stupidity of resorting to physical violence. He had always told us that violence was only to be used in self-defense.

I could tell that, as usual, Rama was using real experiences in the physical world to teach us about Tantric Buddhism, the art of creating positive effects from difficult experiences. Rather than creating bad karma for us, we could take this experience and use it - use the anger and energy we felt to create something that would actually benefit others. Finally, Rama told us his idea. He suggested a big ad campaign to support the book *Surfing the Himalayas*. His answer was to spread the light to counter the darkness.

On the night of the 'Dateline' show, there were a number of parties thrown by students. I went to at least one too many and, forgetting that my college days of hardened drinking were well past, I drank far too much tequila. When I awoke the next morning, I had no idea how I had gotten home. Large portions of the night before were blanked out, and my entire body was telling me I would rather be dead than experiencing the hangover I currently had. I tried to recover all the next day with my intention being to make it to Oracle class that night, a database class offered by Rama. Still, when it was time to prepare for class, I realized that I was going to miss it that week, and rather than risk passing out during class, I would stay in bed and watch a video.

I didn't want to bump into anyone I knew. I was embarrassed to be missing class, and was both looking and feeling like hell. So I waited until class was supposed to have begun and then crawled out of bed, threw on some clothes and drove to the video store. As I drove I suddenly had this idea that I was going to run into Rama, which I really didn't want to do that night given my state of awareness, appearance, and the fact that I was missing class. As a member of two video stores in town, I attempted to figure out which one I thought he was less likely to visit.

I arrived at the store without incident, and picked out one of Rama's favorite comedies that I hadn't seen before. I paid for the video, walked out of the store, and I glanced to my left, still nervous about bumping into Rama. He was ten yards away from me, ambling casually in my direction eating a frozen yogurt, looking straight at me. Cursing my choice of video store, I quickly said, "Hi," and started in the opposite direction towards my car. "Please don't say anything. Please don't say anything," I started praying over and over.

"How's it going?" he asked.

I realized I was going to have to turn to reply, and it occurred to me that having studied with Rama for many years, this was the first time we were going to talk. It was the first opportunity I was going to get to show him the progress I was making in my life. I was depressed, hungover, unshaved and unwashed, in a torn tee shirt, dirty jeans and without socks. Still, since it was my only meeting with Rama, I am now extremely grateful that it occurred. To the best of my recollection this is what we said.

"Great," I lied, turning only half-way in the continued hope that he would let me go.

"Really?" he queried, and continued to walk towards me, obviously indicating I was not free.

"Well, I went to a party last night and had a little too much to drink. What did you think of the show last night?" I impressed myself by having the ability to try and shift the subject off me and onto something neutral.

"Oh, I didn't see it. You know I don't watch those things: they're all the same. But I did get a download afterwards, and I don't think it went too badly. It will probably sell some more books and some more music, and that's a good thing."

We carried on talking for a while about the show, only bits of which I remember, before he came back to me.

"You know you don't look so good."

"I'm sorry to say I'm not feeling so good."

"You know what I see when I see you?" he asked. This, I thought, was an impossible question, and my paranoid mind scanned the possibilities of the scum sucking section in the adjective dictionary that he might be considering.

"No," I replied, chickening out of what I thought he might see.

"I see pride. I see power. I see a bad-ass mother who don't take no crap off of nobody." As he finished the 'Cool Runnings' quote, he punched me in the shoulder and looked deeply into my eyes.

"I see pride. I see power. I see a bad-ass mother who don't take no crap off of nobody." He repeated and punched me again.

"So tell me what I see."

"You see pride. You see power. You see a bad-ass mother who don't take no crap off of nobody," I told him weakly.

"Say it again, but tell me you see it."

17

"I see pride. I see power. I see a bad ass mother who don't take no crap off of nobody."

"That's better," he replied. "So what movie are you getting out?"

At this point I was so relieved both that the subject had changed, and that I had resisted my urge to get an adult movie.

" 'Spaceballs'."

"That is a great choice," he exclaimed. "What's you're favorite part of the movie?"

"Actually I haven't seen it before," I told him.

"Ah, you're going to love it. You know, I used to live next door to Mel Brooks in L.A. He's a very funny guy. Anyway, you have to watch out for the part of the movie where they are watching the movie Spaceballs', within the movie. It's great where they are suddenly watching the exact part of the movie that is going on right then, with Rick Moranis saying how he wants to go back, and they are explaining that they can't. You have to watch out for that bit, it's my favorite part."

"Thank you."

"You're welcome. Good night."

"Good night."

As I walked away, I felt dazed, excited, and thoughtful. I was still hung over, but that no longer mattered, as I was happy.

Rama and I had an ongoing dialog using fortune cookies — hard to believe, but it's true! It went on for years, inspiring, supporting and delighting me.

The first time happened at the beginning of my six years with Rama, in 1992. A large group of new people had just been invited to apply as students, and to go on a special trip to

Hawaii, complete with four dinner seminars with Rama! I was convinced the trip could never happen for me... but I couldn't stop thinking about it.

I'd never had money. Hawaii seemed like an impossible dream. Somehow, though, an inner voice whispered that I could make the money if I really wanted it, really tried.

I picked up some Chinese food on the way home from computer school, and ate it as I talked on the phone with a friend about how much I wished I could go to Hawaii. Then I opened the fortune cookie. "A once-in-a-lifetime adventure awaits you on a South Pacific island." Could this possibly be a coincidence? Do they even make fortunes that say that? My perspective shifted, and I went on the trip, making many changes to do so.

Another especially memorable cookie happened several years later. Things were not going well, and life had lost its brightness for me. I was in a slump. I walked by the Chinese restaurant in the town where I lived and felt I should get some lunch. I almost didn't open the cookie. "I don't believe in fortune cookies anymore," I thought. "I must have been deluding myself." But I opened it anyway.

"The one you love will suddenly appear before you," it read. "OK," I thought, "This is definitely not true, because that would have to mean Rama was going to show up suddenly in my life, and I know that's not going to happen." I went on my grumpy way.

A day or so later, I went for a walk. I left my apartment, where I was working like a maniac to complete something difficult, and strolled aimlessly around my neighborhood, looking at the ground. "The one you love will suddenly appear before you." The fortune ran through my mind, and I looked up. There on the other side of the street, one block from my house was Rama, walking toward me.

We didn't speak. We didn't need to. I believed in fortune cookies again.

I was getting ready for a trip to Italy for a vacation. I was very uncertain about the timing of the trip. Initially, it seemed like a good time to go, but as the date got closer, a bunch of things came up to make me want to reconsider. Opportunities in Rama's program were opening up, I was moving and I had a major deadline at work that I thought I wasn't going to make. During my meditation, I asked Rama to give me a sign one way or another about the trip. I asked him to make it a very obvious sign, so I would not miss it or mistake it for something else. That weekend, we were having a class and Rama was coming to talk to us about the Caribbean trips and show us a scuba diving video. Well, he came in speaking in a heavy Italian accent, "Bonjourno...," talking about trips to the Caribbean. I got my message clearly, and had a very nice trip to Italy.

I once asked Rama how a person could provide their own reality-check for how they were doing with their spiritual practice.

I wanted to ask this particular question on this particular evening, even though I had heard Rama talk about this before. Because he had suggested that we might not have the opportunity to see him for a long while (which, fortunately, turned out not to be true), I wanted to have his answer engraved into my consciousness the way that Rama's answers were, when the question that prompted it was sincere. I also hoped that it might actually be "the question" Rama sometimes waited for one of us to ask, the kind that allowed him to say something that needed to be said.

Rama closed his eyes to listen after acknowledging my raised hand. "In this world, where it is so easy to lie to yourself - for me to lie to myself, I should say, about my spiritual progress..."

Rama interrupted briefly, opening his eyes to look at me sharply, "You've got that right."

I continued, "That being the case, I would like to know, in this period of time when we're trying to get it right on our own, what can I do to basically run a 'self-diagnostic' on myself? How can I do a reality-check on whether I am really on track?"

Rama had kept his eyes open while I finished my question, looking at me in an intent but detached fashion. From the way he held his body, and the way the energy of the room had snapped into a sharp crystalline "moment", I knew it had indeed been a correct question. As he looked into my eyes, all thoughts in my mind slowed down, flattened and shrank, then completely disappeared. Time seemed to stop and I wasn't sure if I was breathing.

"You can only know how you are doing by looking at the level of stillness in your mind and life.

"You have to remember that your outer life and your inner life do not necessarily match. They can be out of sync. You may think that nothing is going 'right' in your life and yet your inner life can be progressing. You can be in a lot of pain, but if you have a balanced perspective, you are going in the right direction. You can tell how you are really doing, internally, by seeing if you are at peace with yourself. If, no matter what, you can maintain control; if, every day, you are feeling a greater peace and stillness – then you are making progress."

This was not quite the answer I was expecting. While Rama had always said that inner stillness was the primary barometer of one's practice, he had also suggested that seeing changes in one's outer life would make it clear that inner changes had been made. Now he was suggesting that, while "being on a roll" indicates that one has "lined up the dots", the contrary is not necessarily true – that one can actually be making inner progress without it manifesting externally. Without going into details, this answer perfectly suited where I was both internally and externally.

"Change happens gradually. It's not about the kundalini rush – that's fun, but don't think it has anything to do with real spiritual growth. Lots of energy rushing around doesn't change you.

"Like the *Dhammapada* says, purity grows drop by drop, impurity grows drop by drop. Small choices make the difference. You have to read the spiritual books, take care of yourself physically, eat a low-fat diet, hassle the details. You have to keep your spirits up. Be optimistic always.

"If your mind is getting more still, no matter what is happening on the outside, you are making spiritual progress.

"The questions to ask yourself are: am I feeling better, am I feeling more equilibrium, am I at peace with myself? Just remember, it happens drop by drop."

One evening Rama took all of the people who were working in his software company out to dinner at a restaurant. Rama sat at the head of a very long table. One guy asked, "How can I learn to meditate really well?" Rama replied, "You have to find something about it that you really like."

During 1992, I was teaching some introductory meditation classes in the Philadelphia area and had met some young people I thought would enjoy spending an evening with Rama. I invited a young man and a young woman to come to a black tie formal dinner that Rama was hosting at the old Mark Twain estate in Westchester County in New York. After the dinner, Rama was going to give a talk and meditate.

The young man was Indian-American and while he was already somewhat versed in Hindu texts and meditation from his own studies exploring his heritage, he was rather startled to be asked to wear a tuxedo. Knowing he was a struggling college student, I arranged to help him with the rental fee for the tux since he was coming as my guest.

He was quite curious about why we would be dressing so formally for an evening of meditation with a teacher. I had explained that in many Buddhist countries it is the custom to put your best foot forward with a teacher. Since this was Rama's first incarnation as an Enlightened teacher in the West in a Caucasian body (he had had numerous incarnations as an Enlightened teacher in various Eastern countries), Rama was adapting to Western customs; hence, a black tie formal dinner followed by a dharma talk and meditation.

I had arranged with both of them to meet me at my house. One of my friends who was teaching in another city was going to drive up and leave her car at my house, and come up the rest of the way with us. My teaching friend arrived, and the young woman also showed up. Then we began to wait. And wait. And wait.

The young man was clearly late. I called his house. His mother, a very gracious lady, said she knew he had been to pick up the tuxedo, so we both knew he was still interested in coming. Neither of us could quite figure out what was happening, as he normally was a very responsible person.

He had driven out very close to my house, but there had been some confusion with the directions. His mother knew we were still waiting for him, which was good, as he thought we would probably leave without him. When he showed up back at his house, his mother let him know we were still waiting. I told him I would come pick him up and bring him to my house as I didn't want to risk any more problems with directions.

By now, it was very late. It was also rather hot. We decided to at least get on the road in our regular clothes as my car did not have a working air conditioner and change into our formal clothes along the way.

We stopped at a way station and made the switch in clothes. We were all surprised how fine everyone looked in their formal clothes and laughed at how funny it was to walk into the way station in our jeans and come out in gowns and a tux.

By now it was really late. We were all very hungry, since we had all eaten lightly that afternoon in anticipation of the formal dinner. In the car, everyone was quiet and hungry. Then one person piped up, "Isn't this just the best salad you've never had?"

We all laughed. We were all thinking about the fact that the dinner was starting without us. "Yes," someone said, "and aren't the flowers you're not seeing just beautiful?" We laughed even more.

And so began our "Zen dinner" experience, as we drove along and laughed at each course that we weren't having, politely doing the dinner conversation for the dinner we weren't eating. It was very festive and funny. With our minds, we were fully focused on enjoying this dinner that we weren't having.

I knew Rama was sending us energy, and I could see it manifesting as the good mood of the passengers grew and grew. By the time we had crossed over the Tappan Zee Bridge into Westchester County, we had already had a virtual dinner. I was hoping we could slip in quietly at the back and find some empty chairs to settle in for Rama's talk.

However, when we entered the mansion and began to go through registration, a tall, curly-haired man in a tuxedo came over and said to my young friends reassuringly, "I knew you were coming, so I had them hold dinner."

I was quite stunned at the courtesy of this. The young man nodded with ease and acted as if this kind of thing happened for him every day.

Then he turned to me and asked, "When will we get to see Rama?"

I smiled, "You just did."

"HIM? I thought he was the head waiter!" the young man exclaimed.

I had to explain to them that no, I hadn't called ahead and told anyone we were coming late, that an Enlightened teacher had felt them coming long distance and had arranged for them to have their dinner, even though we had showed up so late.

So then we went in and had our actual dinner, which turned out to be even better than we had imagined. Rama stopped by our table and made small talk about the music (he was previewing a rock album by Zazen that night) and double-checked to make sure everyone was enjoying their food. I was very touched by his kindness to us.

One of Rama's one-liner sayings was, "I sweat the details." He really lived that.

One night in 1988, when we were living in Westchester County, New York, Rama held a meeting for people who wanted to train to become meditation teachers. He had just dissolved a program for people who wanted to write software, saying the time wasn't right. Many people had signed up to be in both groups, but six of us who had signed up for only the software group went to the meeting for future meditation teachers, figuring we would give it a try.

However, Rama spotted the six of us and questioned whether teaching meditation was what we really wanted to do. We sort of hung our heads in embarrassment at being busted. I personally thought it was way beyond my reach to try to teach meditation, but it seemed really difficult to admit that to someone who obviously loved teaching meditation more than anything, as if I weren't being enthusiastic about his project.

Out loud I said very bluntly, "I'm confused." Rama smiled graciously and said this was a good thing to be. Rama looked us all over and said, "You guys really want to write code," and he playfully moved his hands as if he were nerding out at a keyboard. When I saw that motion, I nodded my head. Sitting at a computer all by myself, working away, yup, that was for me.

Rama had us gather around him in a little group. He said to us in a more private tone that he could tell we were supposed to go out that night and have fun. He pulled out his wallet and reached into it and brought out a crisp $100 bill. He said he wanted to treat us, that we should go out and have pizza and catch a movie and have fun. He kept saying that we were to go have fun.

All six of us just stood there, looking pretty amazed. Here we had come reluctantly, dragging our feet, trying to do "the spiritual thing", and instead we were being spun out to get pizza and go have a blast. I was standing closer to him than some of the others, so I went ahead and took the $100 bill from his hand because I could tell he was sincere about this. I could also tell it was shocking all of us to be taking money from an Enlightened teacher. This really seemed out of the norm. We were suddenly in very uncharted territory as the evening had taken a most unexpected turn.

The six of us left the room, and when we were out of it, we stopped and looked at each other: three men, three women. We unanimously concurred that we had to be really careful how we spent the money, and a couple people even thanked me for taking the $100 bill from him because we had all just been standing there stupidly, not believing what was happening.

We very carefully decided on a pizza place one of the guys knew about near the train station. We went there and ordered pizza and cokes and started to loosen up a bit. We broke the $100 bill paying for the food and then looked at all the change we still had. There was a lot of money left over. It was a pretty funny assignment, and it was even more funny watching everyone start to seriously throw themselves into having fun. If we were spending money from our teacher, we had better be doing things properly. We tried to be very courteous to the people working at the counter, as they were part of our adventure.

We sat at the picnic tables inside the pizza place as we ate the pizza, and someone got a newspaper. We scanned the movie ads to follow our next instruction. We sipped cokes and seriously considered the karmically charged question: which movie would the six of us have the most fun at? We looked for the silliest movie we could find. We settled on a move that was a remake. I could not believe the title, but when someone said it out loud, we all broke out laughing, and that settled it as being the omen we should follow.

We were going to take money from an Enlightened teacher and go see The Blob and have fun. We got pretty high laughing about this. In fact, we got uproarious.

In a merry mood, we drove to the Sawmill Theater in Hawthorne and purchased our tickets. There was still a mountain of change left over. A few people went to save seats, and the rest did the concession line. Then we all got settled in to watch the previews with the popcorn, drinks and candy. And there was STILL an awful lot of money left over.

The movie itself had us laughing many times. At the end of it, we were commenting among ourselves that we weren't sure if the movie was really that funny or if Rama had just spun us so high that we would have giggled at the credits. And then, sure enough, we saw something that made us giggle even during the credits.

We were very aware that our good humor was from an incredible amount of happy energy sent to us from our teacher. We felt good just being together. It was a very innocent humor pervading our consciousness. It was a very easy evening, totally magical.

After The Blob, we went to a nearby diner, and we encountered the most awesome waitress who introduced us to the most extraordinary New York diner deserts. We ordered an enormous amount of dessert and coffee.

We speculated about what our past lives together might have been to have brought us to such a moment, and what in the world kind of karma we had just generated taking money from an Enlightened teacher.

Everybody sparkled all through the dessert. At the end, we left a huge wad of cash, everything that was left over (after the bill was paid), as a tip for the awesome waitress and as a gesture to the spirit.

It was cool to get up and walk away, having done our job and completed our assignment. Rama had dramatically taught us that sometimes "having fun" is the right thing to be doing and is a way for fellowship feelings to blossom.

Rama took a group of guys and gals out to dinner at a Japanese restaurant one night. It was an open forum for any kind of conversation. We talked about everything ranging from Rutger Hauer movies, to the computer industry, to spiritual topics. One guy at our table took the opportunity to ask Rama about mindfulness.

"Rama," he said, "what exactly is mindfulness? I have read about it in so many spiritual books, but I still don't know what it really means."

Rama put his right hand on his chin and contemplated how to answer his student's question so that he might understand. Then he explained, "Well, you know when you really have to take a piss? I mean you really have to pee? You're standing in front of the urinal with your zipper down, and it doesn't matter what is happening in that bathroom, or who is standing at the urinal next to you. All you can think about is taking that piss and nothing else."

The student nodded his head.

"Good," Rama said. "That's mindfulness."

The guys at the table all looked at each other with understanding.

There was a pause as Rama looked around the table. "I see that the gals here need another example. Let's see. Okay. You're in the back seat of a car getting it on with a guy - really hot and heavy. The car is rocking, the windows are steamed up, you're really turned on...and a cop knocks on the car window. Mindfulness means that you have the orgasm anyway."

And the gals at the table all smiled at each other with understanding.

I was working in Toronto and commuting twice a month back to Westchester when the *Surfing the Himalayas* book came out. The first book-signing was announced for Boston during the week, and I thought I couldn't possibly make it. A message went out the night before the book signing, which said that anyone who could get to Boston should go to it. Our support would counteract another group who planned to protest the book's release. It took me about two minutes to make up my mind to go. I bought an airline ticket, called in to work and caught an early flight into Boston.

It was really nice to see the big turnout. Unfortunately, the bookstore and publisher were caught unaware by the crowd and didn't have enough books on hand to sell. Luckily, I had brought the copy of *Surfing the Himalayas* that Rama had given me. I was one of the last people in line to have my book signed, and as I presented it to him for signing, I said, "They ran out, but I have a backup." He looked at me and said, "That's what it's all about, isn't it?"

Sometime at a seminar in the Spring of 1988, Rama asked us what were the "best" shampoos. As I recall it, he didn't specify what he was looking for, at first, and simply let a few people respond. People called out their favorite shampoo brands, many of them well known from years of advertising. After a few attempts, he qualified his question. "When I ask 'what is the best shampoo?' I don't mean what sells the most or which have the marketers convinced people is the best. I mean, what are the best shampoos to use – and what that means is – which shampoos have the best vibe?" Fewer people answered now, with more thought in between. He agreed with far fewer choices than he disagreed with, but in the end there were four or five brands that he considered had a good "vibe" to them.

"Maybe they're made from better ingredients, maybe the company is in a better location, maybe the workers care more about what they're doing – who knows why they're different," he said. "The point is you guys and gals hear me talking about everything you do being part of the process, and you don't understand when I say 'everything,' I mean 'everything.' Everything has a vibration. Everything you use on your body or take into your mouth vibrates at a certain frequency – just like every person and place does. If you want to vibrate at the highest rate yourself, you avoid going to places that vibrate more slowly than you. If possible, you spend the least amount of time with people who would slow you down. Now you should start thinking about commercial products the same way."

The important thing wasn't the particular brands he was mentioning. "Tomorrow, next week, next year – who knows? The same brands might well not come out on top. You will have to, if it matters to you, keep track of this. Don't expect me to come back in a year and give you an update."

Rama, who had been standing during most of this dialog, sat down. After a few minutes, he said, "Of course, you are free to believe this is important or not. You don't have to believe me on any of my choices. I recommend you go check it out for yourself. In Buddhism, it's all based on your own experiences, right? But if you were smart, you would understand that even if this sounds like fluff, it's very important."

At a Solstice event in 1992, Rama told his students, "If you succeed in learning humility, you will have accomplished something in this life." He said that to expect to become Enlightened in this life, though theoretically possible, was unrealistic, due to the actual level of interest demonstrated by his students, and that, in any case, one could not hope to advance at all if one hadn't learned humility. Pretending to be, or mistakenly believing one is focused on Enlightenment without humility is futile. You have to take care of first things first.

On the evening of Rama's birthday, our teaching group had dinner at a fabulous Japanese restaurant in San Francisco. Rama was not with us. He was sponsoring a dinner for a group of students in another city. In honor of his birthday, each of us shared a special moment. The experience I shared was driving to work that day.

> "The morning was very clear, bright and sunny. However, in front of me, unusual clouds were forming. Then an image entered my mind. The heavens and all the Buddhas that have been, were, and were to be, were celebrating Rama's birthday! A feeling of gratitude engulfed me; gratitude for being alive, for what did and did not exist in my life, and for another chance to work with Rama."

Those feelings were still present, even then at dinner. We went around the table continuing to tell stories. We all felt that Rama was there celebrating with us although he was on the East Coast. As the evening progressed, only happiness, laughter and smiles existed in the room. Even the waitress couldn't stop laughing and smiling.

The next day, our group had our regular meeting. Our secretary relayed something to us.

She said, "Someone that attended last night's dinner on the East Coast, hosted by Rama, wanted to share this with us." That "something" would stun all of us.

As she looked around, she conveyed these words, "At one point during the evening, Rama paused while he was speaking. Everyone waited to see what else Rama would say or do. Then suddenly he said, 'Right now, this very moment, the other San Francisco group is having dinner, enjoying each other's company, enjoying life, taking nothing for granted. Each one of them is grateful for their life. It's a perfect moment. One perfect moment, of many perfect moments that make up their lives, that make up each of our lives. Always remember, every moment is perfect and wonderful even in times of hardship or tragedy.'"

Once Rama called me on the phone to discuss a project. It was always wonderful to have a chance to speak to Rama or hear him speak in a seminar, because his optimism and outrageous sense of humor were very contagious, and one couldn't help feeling inspired and uplifted after such an encounter. He also understood human nature very well, and was able to help his students find better ways of understanding and handling all kinds of situations in their lives.

On this particular occasion, he asked me what I had been thinking about lately. I wasn't aware of anything particularly insightful or interesting that had been occupying my thoughts, but I was aware that I had been feeling more *consolidated* lately. He explained, "You are beginning to understand 'having to believe'. You remember that conversation where Don Juan tries to explain 'having to believe' to Carlos [Casteneda], right? You're beginning to see that studying with me is difficult, and life itself is difficult – meaning there are no guarantees! In the beginning it *seems* like everything will work out, but that's just youth. The real work of self-discovery is definitely not easy. This isn't Hollywood where everything works out. But that doesn't mean it never works out! That's where 'having to believe' comes in. It's not 'the power of positive thinking' – that's a nice idea, but it's not what Don Juan is referring to. What 'having to believe' really means is you see that you have *equal* chances of failing as you do succeeding, but you believe beyond a shadow of a doubt that you WILL succeed no matter what the obstacles are. When the warrior really sees this, he does absolutely everything to ensure his success, meaning he lives a tight life and does everything he knows he's supposed to do - all the things his teachers tell him. Of course even this won't guarantee success, but it makes it *possible*. That's the point. You are forced to make an *inner* decision to succeed, and you have to believe it totally, even though you know you might fail! Otherwise it won't work because it won't motivate you to do the necessary things. That's the trick. That's 'having to believe'!"

I met Rama for the second time at an Indian restaurant. A group of new people had been invited to dinner, where we had the opportunity to ask him questions. At the time, we were reading our first recommended book, by Carlos Castaneda, and I wanted to know whether Don Juan was more 'Enlightened' than Don Genaro.

Rama replied, "When you're standing on the ground, looking up at two very tall buildings and you can't see the top of either, does it really matter which one is taller?!"

This is a fantastic occurrence that I will always treasure. I dreamt that I saw Rama at a social function and that he shook my hand. This was a very unusual and memorable dream, because Rama rarely shakes hands with people. Oddly enough, the next night I bumped into someone who invited me to a restaurant where the musician Joaquin Lievano was playing. The restaurant was crowded, and I could find a seat only near the entrance, away from the band. While I sipped on a glass of wine, Rama walked towards me and asked me how I was and then shook my hand. For the first time in my life, I felt what it means to have your breath taken away, and know how ecstatic and beautiful it is to be near or to be touched by an Enlightened Master.

Rama realized that his students, for the most part born into a Western culture where the traditions about teachers, teachings and Enlightenment are so different from the East, were at a real disadvantage in understanding the dynamics involved in a true teacher-student relationship. He could see that there was some critical factor in understanding how to interact with him that we were missing or misunderstanding, and every once in a while, he would stop to explain it to us very patiently.

To the best of my recollection, one night he said, "You think that this is what I am, and when you come to see me, whether you and I are talking one-on-one or you are listening to me give a talk, you think that that is what it's all about. This is a big mistake. You have to remember that you are dealing with two Ramas here." He held up his hand with two fingers extended. "There's this personality that was born in this body, and you like what I have to say or you dislike what I have to say or whatever, but that's not where things are really happening. There's this body, and then there's the energy field that surrounds me that contains the aura of Enlightenment, and that is the true me.

"When you come into contact with the energy field by being here with me, by listening to a tape or reading a book, or by thinking about me, that's when things really happen. That energy field - the body of light - amplifies whatever you bring into it or touch it with. Bring your brightest, happiest thoughts, and they will be amplified. Bring and hold onto your worries and what makes you unhappy, and you will become even more unhappy. Bring your upsets and let them go, and you will move from unhappy to happy.

"It's very simple, really. Stop thinking about me as this body and this personality. What you really want to remember is the aura, how to connect with the aura of an Enlightened Being, and how to bring to it your very best. You don't have to be perfect to connect with this aura. Just bring it the best you can. Stop being so concerned about 'this Rama' and whether he talked to you tonight or what he said or what tone he used. Remember always that what's important in our relationship is your connection with 'that Rama'."

Rama used to invite his students on hiking trips as a way to impart Buddhist empowerments and mystical experiences. On the Spring Equinox of 1994 he arranged a hike in a national park in upstate New York. It was a crisp and sunny morning. The park was surrounded by plush, green, forested hills that were beautiful in the shining sun. By 10:00 am about 350 students were present at the meeting place. Everyone was eager for Rama to arrive and start the "show" (he always entertained as well as empowered his students). Everyone was excited to see Rama, and smiles abounded on the hikers' faces.

Around 10:30 Rama rolled up in his shiny black Mercedes. I whispered out-loud to myself, "Wow, now that's a nice car." Rama popped out of the car dressed in black shorts and a tee shirt. I couldn't help but notice how powerful his legs were. They were long and slender but packed with muscle like a champion marathon runner. He walked into the center of the parking area, and the students all gathered around him in a circle. He greeted everyone with funny jokes and comments that made us all laugh. Right before starting off on our hike, he mentioned that high and beautiful dimensions were opening and closing around us. A powerfully bright and happy feeling surrounded the group as Rama led us towards the woods.

Rama was marching ahead of us at a brisk and consistent pace. I could hear pockets of laughter and giggling throughout the long line of hikers. I noticed some of the more sedentary students having a little trouble keeping up. We hiked through woods and over hills for about an hour, before stopping on top of a thickly forested hill.

Rama stood near the top of the hill as the group sat surrounding him in a horseshoe fashion. He entertained us by telling jokes and poking fun at us while we waited for everyone to make it to the top of the hill. I remember Rama mentioning that if we found the hike to be strenuous, we were not getting enough exercise. When everyone finally made it to the top and found a place to sit, Rama started talking about various topics. I cannot remember the details of the conversation, but a lot of it hovered around career, computer science, and occult Buddhist topics. He told us that this particular hill was a 'power spot' which was just as powerful as many of the power spots that he took his students to in the deserts of the Southwestern United States.

At one point he was taking questions and inviting comments from his students. I piped up and mentioned something about my experience trying to keep mindful throughout the day. Rama acknowledged what I said, and then he addressed what was happening to me internally. He did this all of the time – anyone who asked Rama a question was exposed to a potential internal critique by Rama. Sometimes he would answer a completely different question from the one that was vocalized, one that the person's being was silently asking. Rama looked at me slyly and said, "So you like my car, huh. YOU should be driving a car like that." This response was totally unexpected. I was awestruck as the realization sunk in that Rama read a thought I had an hour ago. I felt an unseen power surround me and fill me with blissful feelings as Rama smiled at me. I knew that the car meant nothing of spiritual value, but was an outer indication of inner Buddhist attainment. Rama had taught me that by successfully applying the Buddhist techniques he was teaching to my inner-life, success in my outer-life was inevitable.

This casual conversation between Rama and his students continued for several minutes. At one point in this enchanted meeting, Rama's tone turned serious. When Rama taught he inspired. Like all Buddhist Masters, he also critiqued his students when they were acting in selfish and destructive ways. As he was critiquing us he looked right at me. My thoughts stopped cold, and I was transfixed by his stare. Rama was in super-focus as he talked. As his tone became more intense everything around me started blurring into light. This continued until I could no longer see anyone or anything around me accept Rama. He literally lifted my consciousness out of the physical world into a world of light. His tone was severe, and all of the things that he said rang true. After a few timeless moments in this state, I saw the light around me slowly form back into my friends and the surrounding forest. As the truth of his comments settled in to my consciousness, Rama made a wisecrack and broke up the tension of the moment. Rama chatted lightheartedly with us for a few more minutes before starting the hike back to where our cars were parked.

By the time we got back I felt energized and, despite the criticism Rama imparted to us, felt that I had not a care in the world. Rama had a way of combining light and humor with correction, so that all we felt was inspired.

One of my first jobs in New York City was as a temporary secretary at a medical clinic. I was right out of college and had only been studying with Rama for a short time. At this office one of the employees was a young woman whom most people in the office thought was very nice. And she seemed to be, to everyone except me. There was something about her that annoyed me all the time. In my opinion she was a simple, typical girl from Brooklyn who would get married, have kids and enjoy her weekends at the mall. I could not see the value of her life or how she could be much better than a robot, never bothering to question the deeper mysteries of life.

I knew my attitude and thoughts were incorrect and shallow towards her. Rama taught us that true spiritual seekers always love each life as their own. But the moment my 2-D colleague would walk in the room, I would get tremendously annoyed. My haughty attitude was driving me crazy. So I made it a habit to run to the ladies' room and attempt to meditate whenever I got out of control with my thoughts.

While on the toilet one day, trying to enter a deep meditation which would clarify my views and mind, it occurred to me that what I really needed to do was rise above my own ego. But it seemed to me that in order to do that I'd have to go into samadhi or something, which essentially meant becoming Enlightened. This would not help my current situation, as I didn't think Samadhi would happen at that particular moment.

A few days later Rama held a seminar in Westchester County, just north of New York City. There were approximately 300 people in the seminar room that night. To my surprise, as if Rama knew, he started talking about humility, the exact thing I had been struggling with all week!

He said that up until that time, he had only told two, maybe three people, the true secret to humility. Rama stated that the true secret to humility was, "Don't care." It was because I cared how the woman at my office chose to live her life and exist that she had the power to drive me crazy. Rama said that when you care about things they gain power over you. This did not mean not to respect life, be kind and love things, but rather to love without the sense of possession or attachment. At a later time Rama also said that a good example of humility in a person was shown by a character played by Kevin Costner in the movie "The Bodyguard".

As Rama continued speaking, easily holding my complete attention, he suddenly started talking about different dimensions one can reach in their meditation, and told us he was going to show us an astral dimension. As he spoke the room began to lose its solidity and glow with a very soft light. After a minute in that dimension, he announced that he was going to take us to a still higher astral dimension, and the room simultaneously became less solid and brighter. I tried to pay attention in order to remember what these dimensions felt like so I could get back to them in my own meditations. Then Rama announced he was going to take us above our ego and self by lifting us to a causal dimension.

'No way!' I thought in shock. Was it really possible to get above self and ego in a causal dimension? You don't have to enter into Nirvana to be above your ego? I was really excited now, as the room became extremely viscous with light. It was as if every particle in the room, my body and my mind just became unlocked from its fixed position and began to glow and vibrate. Then, while in that causal dimension, I had the realization that I could not pay attention to this dimension like I had the other two. Not because I wasn't aware, but because there was no "me" there. Where Rama had just taken me, there was no self anymore.

In my dream I was a professor, giving a presentation in front of a whiteboard. I was drawing a complicated relationship between two financial instruments. One had a very high yield, and the other had fairly low returns. When combined into a single package, the return on these instruments was not an average of the two: it was actually less than the average. This was due to some statistical property that I understood very well in the dream. By not combining the two instruments, the one with the higher returns would actually produce exponentially higher returns on its own.

In retrospect, I realized that what I was really drawing was the result of the relationship which I had just ended with my long-time boyfriend.

After I concluded the presentation of my research, I turned to face the audience. The only person in the room was a very sophisticated man, appraising the lecture. He was leaning back casually in his chair, wearing academic-looking glasses. It was Rama. "Well, Professor," he said, "it looks like you hit the dick on the head!"

Rama had never mentioned the word "initiation" before tonight. But as the energy crackled at the end of a National Personal and Professional Development Seminar (NPPDS) in D.C., he explained what it meant. He said that this event would be a special empowerment, but we had to make certain that we were ready for it. We had to choose whether we were ready for this next level — or not. And he said that this decision would be karmically binding. That evening as we were sitting in a room with Rama, the energy was so intense you could cut it with a knife. And believe me, it did feel like the entire sum of my incarnations was right there in the room with me.

I had been coming out of a rather rough time. I had just moved to D.C. from Palo Alto, California, where I had spent six difficult months. It was the second cross-country trip I had taken in a year. I had been out of computer school for a couple of years, but I was still trying to nail down that first "real" job. Although I was looking forward to the new start in D.C., I felt a certain heaviness. Even though I had eagerly signed up in the past for new adventures, this new commitment scared me.

Rama said that he would make it easy for us...he would give the word, and anyone who stood up would be initiated. Anyone who was still sitting had silently made their choice to end their journey with him. He asked if we were ready, and a room full of bright, excited people shook their heads and smiled.

In this deciding moment, he calmly said, "Those who wish to be initiated, please stand." It seemed as though the room came to its feet. There were rare smatterings of people that remained seated, but they were few and far between. I tried to stand, but I felt a sensation like a weight on top of my head, pushing me into the floor. I wondered if my legs would support me if I tried to stand, but that seemed impossible. The energy in the room intensified as Rama initiated the standing multitude. I heard Rama say to the new initiates, "You realize that by doing this, you are willing to have your picture on the front page of the New York Times!" Nervous, excited giggles rippled through the audience. I thought that I was willing to do that, to tell the world that I was his student, but I was still sitting! Maybe I didn't have what it takes after all.

As if feeling that the energy had reached its peak, he said, "OK...good... please sit down."

It was too late...I had failed.

I couldn't believe it. I had come all of this way, just to quit now? Was this really what dharma had in mind for me? I felt crushed.

Rama made some perfunctory business announcements and wished well those who had chosen to leave. Then he bid us goodnight.

I stayed in my seat as happy, smiling faces left the room with their new empowerment. I was glued to my chair; I just couldn't leave yet. The gal giving me a ride asked me if I was ready to go. I asked her to wait; I told her that I had something important to do. She seemed to realize the seriousness in my demeanor and agreed to meet me outside.

A small line of people was already forming at the front of the room, waiting to talk to Rama. I joined at the end of the line. Maybe it was my anticipation, or maybe it was the time, but the line seemed to take forever. I tried to be respectful and not overhear previous conversations, private moments with Rama. Some were obviously saying goodbye. I wondered what I would end up saying to him.

As the number of people preceding me in line decreased, I could feel the intensity of his aura increased. I knew that, occasionally, people would go up and ask a frivolous question of Rama, just to get some attention. I am embarrassed to say that I was one of those people once in a great while — but tonight, as Rama would say, "The power was up." I knew that this had better be important. On this night, I felt that my life, even my future incarnations, were on the line.

Finally, my moment had come. I looked up at the platform where Rama sat in a big chair. I was almost startled — he was breathtaking in appearance. The bright golden light bathed his body like pictures of the Buddha. He sat there like the wise old sage, ready to hear the pupil's query. In energy and appearance, he seemed to be ten times larger than usual. The light that surrounded him was so bright; I could hardly see his physical body. And as I stood there that night, looking up at him on the platform, he looked magnificent.

He looked at me curiously and asked, "What can I do for you?"

I was nervous, but I had to choke the words out. Was he going to tell me that I had already made my choice...that it was too late...that it was my dharma to leave?

"I think that I made a terrible mistake," I said in an apprehensive voice.

"And what was that?" his voice boomed in the empty room.

"When you did the initiation, I didn't stand up...and I was wondering if I could change my mind?" I said timidly, hoping that I didn't sound too stupid.

Time seemed to stand still as he smiled and looked down at me, "My child, don't you know that this is Oz?" His hand motioned gracefully as though he was showing me the Emerald Palace.

My heart melted.

"Do you want to do this?" His eyes were evaluating whether I was genuine.

"Yes!" My voice sounded surprisingly resolute.

He closed his eyes to meditate for a moment. I automatically closed my eyes too. The light that seemed impossibly bright became brighter.

A moment later, his eyes opened, "It's done." Without fanfare, he nodded his head for my dismissal. But we both knew what really happened.

"Thank you, thank you very much," I said quietly. My eyes started to fill with tears. I had to get out of there before I embarrassed myself. I felt the heavy weight being lifted off of my shoulders. He nodded his head again and gave me a small smile. I turned around and practically skipped back down the aisle.

I walked in the cool night to meet my ride, and I felt like anything was possible.

One bright afternoon in March Rama invited me to go shopping. I met him at a local shopping center, and we headed out for a furniture store to look at couches. Once we reached the freeway and ran into the Friday afternoon traffic, however, he immediately changed course and drove instead to a small clothing boutique.

As we walked from the car to the store, Rama explained that I should look around for clothing that would be appropriate for him to wear to meetings with us. It was an exercise in seeing. He explained that meetings, for him, were like public performances or a show, and the clothing he wore was specifically for a particular performance.

Once inside the boutique, I walked all around, examined the things hanging in every square inch of the store, and came up with only one jacket. Rama found about fifteen items. He showed them to me one at a time, and even then I did not see what it was about most of them that made him choose them. The look of a few, in fact, was very unusual, very edgy.

Rama also let the saleswoman help him review each garment while I stood by. Social skills not being my strong point, he pointed out to me quietly and briefly that I should notice his interactions with her; how he let her do what she was best at, allowing her shine in her area of expertise, which, he said, was to show him how each article was best suited and worn by him. He asked her opinion several times, and he was courteous and appreciative of her comments and suggestions. At one point, after she adjusted something on him, he walked over and drew my attention to the fact that he had adopted the attitude women have when trying on clothes. He said he had done this because women tend to be open to help and suggestions while men generally aren't, and it was less abrasive for her to interact with that energy.

After some time, he selected a few things to buy and included the jacket I had picked without question or review. It was another example of his etiquette.

As we drove home, I asked how I could learn to see better. He was looking straight ahead, driving, as he replied, "Always follow brightness."

Rama was planning a series of public meditations for several major cities in America. We were living in Los Angeles at the time, by the beach in Malibu. Rama asked us to go and put up posters in some of the cities a few weeks before each seminar. He'd been doing public meditation for years, and had always found that putting up posters was one of the best advertising methods. So we were planning a trip to Denver.

We had gotten the posters, and studied the maps and the Yellow Pages. We were looking for places to put up posters - bookstores and martial arts studios and health food stores. Friday night we had a meeting at a big house to discuss the details. We were talking about the weather (a big snowstorm was due out of the Rocky Mountains), and what sections of Denver and Boulder to focus on. Right then a black 4-wheel drive vehicle drove into the driveway. Rama hopped out and strode into the house. He walked to the living room where we were, sat down on the couch and talked about meditation.

At one point he closed his eyes, and we all sat meditating. "Where are we?" he asked.

The room had become very still. There was an ancient feeling. The energy was shimmering gold.

"Tibet," said one guy. Rama shook his head.

"Japan," said another. Another shake.

Rama waited a moment and then said, "India. Don't you remember? We used to sit up all night. It was very hot. I remember the shutters on the windows." He smiled. "I remember the shutters. This is India. India is timeless."

It was the spring of 1996, on an otherwise normal afternoon of working for Rama in the software business, when he walked into the office and was about to pass me in the hallway. As he passed by I heard a shrill war cry, and while I was still identifying the totally unexpected sound, I realized that my testicles had been seized in a viselike grip. Frozen and shocked, I seemed to be reacting in slow motion. Finally, I could see Rama's face smiling mischievously, just a few inches from my own. When our eyes met he released me and laughed uproariously in that unforgettable deep baritone.

As I struggled to catch my breath, I realized that I was completely unhurt. He continued laughing unabated, and then, almost in tears, he finally said, "You've got to be ready at all times!"

At a dinner in 1994, when I first met Rama, he talked about the Enlightenment process. He said that as you start to go through the Enlightenment cycle, kundalini energy begins to flow through your body at an incredible rate. There's nothing you can do about it. You can't stop it, and it's extremely painful physically. Rama told us that when it was happening to him, he used to dread going to sleep at night. He would go to bed and it would start - the Light would just pound through his body. He said it was like getting your period, but it never ends. It just keeps getting stronger and stronger every day. He told us that he became very weak at that time, because the Light was so powerful. He said, "What you have to go through in order to become Enlightened is like what Margaret Thatcher had to go through to become Prime Minister."

I first saw Shanti dancing on the sidewalk on Bancroft Avenue near the Admin building at UC Berkeley. He was something of a fixture there, right at the juncture of Telegraph Avenue. He always dressed in white and wore a knit or crocheted cap, also in white. He could often be seen dancing around, as if to remind us of something about life beyond our books, papers and classes. He also had an eye for women and would often walk beside them as they went by. I tried to avoid him, and was always privately relieved that I was more together than he appeared to be.

Years later, I met Rama and became a student in his program. One night, before a meeting, as I stood in the back of the room surveying the available seating, I was shocked to see Shanti dancing down near the stage. He was wearing the same white outfit. I was dressed in a business suit. I couldn't believe we were in the same room. Eventually Rama came in and sat down.

Still standing near the stage, Shanti said to Rama, "They don't know who you are."

"I know", Rama replied. I wondered what it was they knew.

A few years later, standing on the side of the stage one evening, Rama related a story to us. He told us that Shanti had gone into the hospital for an operation, and Rama had called him on the phone to see how he was doing. Instead of complaining, as many people would have done given Rama's ear at such a time, Shanti sang "Ram Ram Hari Ram Shiva Ram" to him over the phone. As Rama sang the words for us, the sound was so alive and real, and from his face emanated such light, that for a moment I glimpsed how deeply and completely Rama loved God, and I saw that in spite of it being the 1990s in America, these ancient words of love for God were still profoundly valid and real.

I realized then that Shanti had a level of understanding I didn't; he shared a love of God with Rama and for Rama, a love that was unafraid and beyond convention.

It was a night in early summer 1996, and Rama had called a meeting of a group of students who were then involved in one of his software projects. Rama arrived wearing the most outrageous, outstandingly beautiful yellow suit - the Versace Spring collection, which he proceeded to model for us, showing off the cut and fabric of the jacket, the matching vest, and of course his new Versace watch! Everything about him that night was gold!

Over the course of the evening, Rama told us a story about his house. He said that when he was looking for a house on the East Coast he visited every beautiful estate in the area. He saw countless gorgeous homes, but didn't really like any of them. Finally, the real estate agents were at their wits' end. They had nothing left to show him, except for this one place. They said it was in really bad shape so he really wouldn't want to waste the time seeing it. Naturally, Rama insisted on seeing the place, even though it was in a state of total neglect and disrepair. In fact, anyone else would have passed it over. But he saw that it had something. That it had potential. So he bought the house, and over the course of the next few years he knocked down most of it, rebuilt it, and completely redid the whole thing. So that now, people who saw it said it was the most beautiful house they had ever seen.

He went on to tell us that we were like that house. Anyone else would have passed us over. No one else would have taken us on. But he could see something in each of us. Something that cannot be put into words. He said, "You each have something. It's different for each one of you. You each have a shine." He told us that his problem was that he fell in love easily. And that he had fallen in love with that little part of each of us (though there was a lot about us he didn't like and wanted to change and completely redo!).

Rama said that if we let him, he would give us such lives, lives so miraculous that we couldn't even imagine, lives that other people didn't even dream were possible!

And then Rama said that no matter what happened, he would always look after us, throughout all of eternity. Then he looked at us and said, "You guys don't know what that means, do you?" And he turned to one of the gals who he had known for a long time and asked her to explain to us what he meant. She said that it meant we would be taken care of on every level forever. Rama nodded. On every level. And the room turned into light.

Rama was many things to many people. He was an Enlightened Being, a teacher, a Siddha Master, a healer, an author, a businessman, a computer expert, a producer, a scuba dive master, a black-belt martial artist. He was all these things and more. Rama regularly redefined who he was, changing in bright and wonderful ways all of the time. He was also a different person for each student he worked with. He would change his demeanor to make people feel comfortable around him or to teach them something by how he behaved or handled a situation. But regardless of who he appeared to be, Rama was perfect all of the time. He was impeccable in every action.

I had the great opportunity to work for Rama at one of his software companies for over a year. During that time, I learned more about business, software, Rama and myself than I ever thought was possible. I had seen Rama in all the aspects that I have mentioned, but this was the first time that I saw Rama as a Warrior Businessman. Fearless, cut-throat, and direct, he tempered his business intensity with extreme fairness and grace in every situation. Having seen Rama give talks on stage and turn golden while in deep meditation, I was surprised and a little bit afraid of this "raw" side of Rama.

One night Rama was trying to inspire us in our business endeavors, and correct some of our mistakes that were costing his business a lot of money. No matter what he said, he couldn't get through to us. In an instant, his aura turned bright red and he knocked a huge vase of flowers onto the floor. He said that he was coming from the place of a Samurai in war. He said that he was slimming down for battle, and he would win his business war with us or without us. He had our attention! He wanted us to shoot for perfection. I remember being in awe of Rama and I internally dedicated myself to Rama's business endeavors, in order to learn from him and advance professionally.

Rama gave us everything we needed to succeed in his businesses. We had extensive training, the necessary materials, Rama's financial backing, and his personal attention when we needed it. Somehow he would always manage to give us his time if we requested it, even though he was the CEO of many businesses and very busy. And he expected something in return for his dedication. Rama wanted to work with people who returned his dedication with their own. He looked at sales numbers, software reports, accounting figures, and legal contracts. Just as in corporate America, when a part of the business was suffering because employees were not performing, he made corrections. One night Rama fired half of his sales team. He read off a short list of salespeople who had made their quotas and said, "The rest of you are fired." Immediately, people complained, expecting the same forgiveness that Rama always exhibited as a meditation teacher. He explained that business was not the same as spiritual education. Business is about getting ahead, making tough decisions, operating in a lean and mean environment with employees who are players. If he made the same exceptions in business that he did in the meditation hall, the whole company would go under. I saw that it was necessary to be that truthful with myself. How many times had I made excuses for my laziness and negativity? How many times had I made an exception to not meditate or study or exercise when I should have? Rama's approach was refreshing to me. I began to see our group as soldiers in his army. He built up a fighting battalion that would go to war for him in corporate America.

And we did go to war in corporate America - for Rama and for ourselves. He created an environment where we could make a lot of money if we applied what he had taught us. We learned to be professional, to apply pressure at the right moments, to negotiate, to be fair, and to believe in ourselves. I watched my fear of business melt away as I tackled assignment after assignment. For the first time, I could really apply the spiritual side of what Rama taught me in a practical way. I would meditate every day to gain clarity in my business deals and the energy to achieve my goals. I exercised to work out tension from the day's problems and to revitalize myself for another day at the office. I applied mindfulness to my daily routine to stay organized and focused. And I learned to be funny, because as Rama always said, "You have to be funny, or you won't last long."

There were times when I wanted to give up, to "throw in the towel" and live a less stressful and more quiet life. But Rama always challenged me to strive for more. One night I decided to quit. I was burnt out and tired. I felt like I couldn't succeed with the structure we had at the office. I made up my mind, packed my briefcase, and made my way to the elevators outside the main office. The elevator doors opened, and Rama stepped out. He smiled brightly and invited me into his office with some other people to celebrate the birthday of one of his managers with chocolate cake. I couldn't say no. He was full of energy and excitement. He was planning a new advertising blitz and was inspecting the brightly colored ads that had just arrived. He raved about how wonderful the products were, and how great it was to be in the software business. Then he stopped. We were all watching him in amazement, surprised that he was so full of life and energy at all times. The room was deafeningly silent. He looked at each one of us in the eyes and said, "Thank you. I know what each one of you is doing for me, for each other and for this company. I appreciate each and every one of you. Thank you." Then he told us to finish our small pieces of cake (you have to watch your calories) and get back to work! How could I give up? His eyes challenged me to outdo myself, to surprise myself by daring to see who I might become if I continued to aim for more.

Business with Rama can be summarized into one word - willpower. Rama taught us that we can achieve anything we want in life if we cultivate and perfect our willpower. We can become millionaires or achieve Enlightenment. We can succeed at anything that we set our minds to. This seems like a simple realization, but it has to be experienced to be believed. A small group of people had dinner with Rama one night to discuss sales strategies and upcoming corporate events. I had had a particularly successful sales month, so halfway through the dinner, Rama asked me to share with the group how I had done it. I could tell everyone was expecting an inspiring pep talk about how I just stayed excited enough to keep going. But I didn't. I explained that each day was a challenge for me, and the only reason I could continue when I was discouraged was through sheer willpower. Rama nodded his head in agreement with what I had said. He told us how difficult it was to complete his last novel. He had to work nonstop for three months to write an entire book while managing all of his companies and maintaining his personal life. He explained that, he too, relied on willpower, which he cultivated through meditation, to continuously succeed at everything he did even when he didn't want to.

Eventually, Rama changed his sales strategy to an Internet-based approach, and we would no longer be working for him as salespeople. Needless to say, most of us were very upset that we would not be working for Rama anymore. I had set up a number of appointments with my clients, so I agreed to complete my final week of sales calls and then move on. I had been on a long tour along the East Coast which concluded in Connecticut where I had my final sales call. My partner and I had perfected our presentation, streamlined our sales tactics, and mastered the art of closing the sales deal. Therefore, what occurred at this final appointment was surprising indeed! We were going through the software's features when our sales prospect asked if it had a certain feature. I said, "Yes!" "And does it have this feature?" he asked. I said, "Yes!" Again he asked, "And this feature?" I said, "Yes, oooohhhh, yes!" And for some inexplicable reason, I began to laugh. And my partner began to laugh. And no matter how hard we tried, we couldn't stop laughing. We laughed uncontrollably throughout the rest of the presentation, which proved to be the most embarrassing hour of my entire life! Our client (he actually bought the software) remarked, "Geez, you guys really love this software!" And I said, "Yes, oooohhhh, yes!" Rama's final business lesson for us was to not take ourselves too seriously.

It took me awhile to realize what Rama was doing for us. Like a physical trainer who creates a personalized program to perfect an individual's body, he created a personalized and complex structure for each one of us to grow spiritually and professionally. He created an arena where we could test out his teachings, and learn to apply them to real life. He pushed us to the edge of our potential, and just before we lost it, he would save us, nurture us, and shove us back out into reality to expand us again.

Some people who knew Rama didn't understand what he was doing. How could business be spiritual? What was all this talk of "business is war" and "you know how you are doing spiritually by how well you succeed in business"? They didn't understand this other side of their teacher. But I am grateful for it. Rama turned us into highly successful business people. He gave us a tangible way to advance spiritually and professionally. We learned how to benchmark our progress in his corporate structure. It wasn't easy. In fact, it was the hardest thing I have ever done. Rama always said that life is the best teacher. Life doesn't lie. Now we are real. And, we have the skills to be successful in life, thanks to Rama.

For a small, meek, nerdy girl who was afraid to use the telephone to call for a pizza in college, climbing her way to the top in the business world was no small feat. Having just submitted a report directly to the CEO of one of the largest insurance companies in the world, she sat back to reflect on how it all came to be. Had it not been for the keen attention of one great man, her life would have never turned out to be this good.

The first time she saw him, dressed in the most stylish late-summer business attire, she thought, "So maybe being corporate wouldn't be so bad after all." Fashion was, in fact, her most important endeavor in life so far. From the way that he dressed, to the way that he walked into a room, to the way that he spoke to a large audience, keeping the attention of each individual, she thought instantly that she wanted to be like him. Calm, cool, more than collected, but angry or loud if the situation called for it, this was someone to emulate.

As with any good mentor, it was not always easy studying business with Rama. His frank comments regarding how she dressed, how she wore her hair, how much she weighed, and how she would (not) spend her spare time, etc. were extremely hard to hear. But, these were all aspects of a career woman's life to which he was molding this young lady. She read many books for Rama's classes on subjects like business administration, science fiction and classic literature - more than she ever thought possible. You see, she had a reading comprehension problem. (Rama's cure for her was to write papers on them too.) Rama also held black-tie dinners at the finest establishments giving her a chance to, at first, humiliate herself, and eventually, feel welcome in the art of fine dining.

Why did she go through ego torture just to be an awesome businesswoman? It was her personal choice. Rama would tell her that she could leave at any time and there would be no hard feelings. Rama meant this, but she knew she couldn't find a better teacher anywhere. She knew he was right. His comments were paying off, literally. She was building up her confidence and her knowledge of business, and this, in turn, was paying her more and more salary each season. Money wasn't the only reward: she found the person inside of her that she always knew she could be. She was running the meetings now.

So when she sheepishly walked in to one of her last meetings with Rama, expecting to receive a disapproving look because she thought she was wearing the wrong eyeglasses for a business situation, she laughed aloud as she looked up and saw he was smiling and wearing the same frames, too.

Rama lived his life with heart. He put his heart into every aspect of it. He lived fully and he lived for his students. He used to say that the greatest reward of being a teacher was watching his students grow.

Shortly after Rama started teaching in the New York area in 1988, he invited his students to dress in their best business attire for a fashion show and critique. A male buddy of mine and I decided to go shopping downtown the next day to try to spiff up our appearance. Neither of us was making a lot of money at the time, and we didn't know much about shopping, especially in New York, so we went to the one store we knew about, Macy's. My friend bought himself a bright new tie in a style that was current, and I got myself a pair of new shoes.

The night of the fashion show came. Each of us went up on stage and Rama critiqued our outfits and businesslike appearance. Some people were told they needed to look less like wallflowers. Others were dressing in a style too flashy for the world of computers.

When it was my turn, I was told, "Your suit is very conservative and conservative looks good on you." That was a relief. My eyeglasses were old and I was told that I needed to get new ones. There must have been more that I don't remember. Then, as I was walking off the stage, Rama had one more comment. "The shoes are great," he said. I smiled all the way back to my seat.

Some time later, my buddy had his turn. There were comments about what was good and what could be improved - I don't remember what they were. And again, just as my buddy was heading off the stage, Rama said, "And the tie. I really like the tie." Rama was like that.

I wanted to apologize to Rama for having screwed up on one of his projects. He stared fiercely, directly into my eyes and said, "The way to put it right is to do it right!"

About three years ago, I was making $7.50 an hour, and I was not sure what I wanted in life. I had so many dreams. One of my dreams was to be a very successful woman. In fact, I could visualize myself wearing a powerful suit, going to work with a smile on my face. It was a dream, but it felt so real...

One day, I received a letter from my sister inviting me to attend one of Rama's seminars. I just packed my things and moved to New York. Even though it might seem crazy, for some strange reason, I knew that was the right thing for me to do. I was so happy and so frightened at the same time. My life started changing the moment I made that decision.

The night of the seminar, the room was full of people I did not know, and I confess that I felt a little uncomfortable. At the same time, excitement was flowing through my veins. Suddenly, there was a silence... Rama was walking in with the biggest smile. I also remember noticing for the first time, his unforgettable way of walking — very casual, yet graceful and deliberate.

Seeing him and feeling his presence that night made me feel as if I were flying. I felt that I had no body anymore. It was amazing to see light actually coming from him and filling the room!! It was magic... Everything became so clear to me.

Rama made my dreams come to reality. He actually taught me to believe in my dreams because they are real. Today I am a successful professional working in the Wall Street area for one of the big six Management Consulting Firms! I am now planning to get my MBA. All of this is thanks to a perfect being who showed me that happiness is stored inside of me all the time. We just need to open ourselves to it by meditating, thinking positive thoughts, and "By being perfect all the time, even though we know that we are not." Everything else comes along with that knowledge. Thanks, Rama. I love you with all my heart and soul.

Rama was the most patriotic person I know. This incarnation was his first in America. Being an Enlightened Tantric Master in the West posed its challenges for Rama. Westerners

51

don't really understand the etiquette of the East, nor do they realize their amazing good luck to have such a being in the West. Nevertheless, Rama loved the principles on which this country was founded - life, liberty, the pursuit of happiness, freedom of speech, and freedom of religion. Rama studied the Constitution and *The Federalist Papers*, he examined the mindsets of our Founding Fathers, and he spoke about the fact that this country was born out of the belief that people should be free to choose their own religion. Rama's family, in fact, had roots in government and the military. One of his relatives landed in the 1st wave of Guadal Canal, another served at Iwo Jima, his brother was a fighter pilot in the Navy, his uncle a police sergeant, and his father once was the mayor in Stamford, Connecticut. So it was natural for Rama to take a special interest in the U.S. government and military when he began selling the advanced, artificially intelligent software products he had designed. Several of his employees had the special opportunity to serve on a team specifically designed to support and cater to these clients. While participating in that team we had the unique opportunity to learn about business, grace, strength, willpower and teamwork from Rama, a Master of business, sales and Enlightenment.

Rama's software products were designed to handle all types of business and technology challenges. These challenges included the Year 2000 problem, networking issues and e-commerce. His government and military clients had even greater challenges. They were dealing with mission critical systems, which control the finances, organization, and the security of this country. What happens, for example, if computers fail for the Department of Defense, or the Federal Aviation Administration, or the FBI? So Rama took his software design and support seriously. He even made special versions of the software, which incorporated governmental standards and special requirements. When we were selected for his government and military team, we knew we had to handle the responsibility with honor and integrity.

We were trained, and the next thing we knew, we found ourselves walking down the Joint Chiefs of Staff hall in the Pentagon, or winding our way to CIA spook sites in the middle of nowhere, or on a Naval base. We even met with people at high security intelligence facilities where we had to wait a week for clearance, take a special car onto the site and relinquish all electronic equipment except for our laptops, which were scanned before we were allowed to enter the building. And they loved Rama's software! Some people bought it on the spot. We sold hundreds of copies to the most sophisticated generals, admirals, and high-ranking government officials around. Purchase orders would flow into the office in multiples every week. They were astonished at how great the software was, and thanks to Rama's training, they were amazed at the service we provided where other software companies simply fell short.

We kept a "war room" where we planned our sales calls, coordinated trainings, and tracked our customers so that no agency was left unattended. We built a board, which had a map of the United States, and the symbol for every U.S. government and military organization that existed at the time. Our war room proudly displayed the flags of the United States, the Army, Navy, Air Force, and Marine Corps. In the end, our team visited practically every government building in Washington D.C., and traveled to every state in America. And they all owned Rama's software. Every single state, every government agency and every branch of the military. Not one organization was overlooked. When Rama read the customer list out to all of us, we were really proud of our team, and we were proud that our boss really cared about his clients and employees.

It is only now that we have completed our mission that we can truly understand and marvel at what Rama was teaching us and doing for his clients. We watched Constitution and Independence Avenues light up with the energy of Enlightenment. We saw how our clients' careers advanced and how their organizations grew as they embraced his technologies. And we were thrilled when they rejected the negative media campaigns, saying that the software was so great they would never give it up. For our part, we grew tremendously. We stood by Rama and we represented Enlightenment when we sold his products. It is impossible to describe the satisfaction and happiness that brought us. On an external level, we grew from corporate novices into senior-level professionals. We have walked confidently in high heels and skirts (we were mostly women) through our nation's most powerful and high-security buildings, into a room of 20 senior military or government officials to present and successfully sell software. Needless to say, we are now capable of handling difficult and complex business situations and command generous six-figure salaries in the corporate world. And we are more patriotic than you can imagine.

When I started attending meditation seminars with Rama, I was working part-time as an administrative assistant and studying to become a massage therapist. The first time I met Rama I knew I had found someone who could really teach me something about life! There was something truly magical and peaceful about him; he was totally at ease with himself and everything around him, even though he was clearly a very powerful person. It was obvious he had figured out how to be successful both spiritually and materially. I felt an incredible energy and clarity whenever I meditated with him during a seminar or even by being in the same room with him. These affects began to spill over into my daily life as I practiced meditation and followed his recommendations, such as meditating and working out daily, studying martial arts, and trying to be mindful during everyday activities. I started to feel very excited and engaged in my life, which wasn't what I expected from a meditation class at all. I realized that I understood very little about spirituality and Buddhism, even though I had practiced self-discovery for several years, because I assumed that being spiritual meant retreating from the world as much as possible. What I learned from Rama is that happiness, fulfillment and spiritual advancement don't come from running away or spacing out; they come from living a grounded, structured life where you consciously engage in the kind of activities that increase your personal power, and avoid the things that decrease it. Rama really emphasized career, specifically a career in computer science, as a means to increase personal power and pursue self-discovery.

I had no technical background whatsoever when I began attending seminars with Rama. I had used a word processor occasionally in college, and I was pretty convinced that was all the technical knowledge I'd ever want or need. For several months I continued to pursue my career in holistic health while attending Rama's seminars. However, since the rest of Rama's recommendations had a really positive effect on my life, outlook, and overall energy level, and his arguments in support of a computer science career sounded very practical, I eventually decided to learn how to work with computers.

I took a six-month programming course at a local technical school, and even though I did better than I expected, I didn't feel ready for my first computer job. Rama recommended that I find another program on the East Coast where I would be looking for my first job. That year I enrolled in another certification course at a local university. I did surprisingly well in all of my programming courses, getting mostly A's. There was one course, however, that was very difficult for me. I'm not sure why it was so difficult, but the professor was one of the worst I had ever had and I was tempted to blame it all on him, but Rama would have none of it. He said, "There's ALWAYS a bad professor – no one goes through school without at least one 'bad' professor, in fact you're lucky to just have one! So now get over it and figure out how you're going to get an 'A' in this class. That's the game in school - 'how many A's can I get?' The point is to keep pushing yourself, otherwise it's no fun." Getting an 'A' in this course seemed like a complete impossibility, and certainly didn't sound like my idea of fun, but I knew I couldn't back down and save face. He recommended getting a tape recorder so I could go over the class lectures at home, several times if necessary, until I understood the material. He told me he had a similar experience in school while working on his Ph.D. The requirements for his doctorate included learning three foreign languages. He chose Russian as one of his languages but for the life of him he couldn't master it. The other languages came fairly easily to him, but in order to learn Russian he had to get a tutor and study harder than he did for his other language courses combined. So he told me to get tutoring and get my tape recorder, and study the material every single day until I absolutely knew it. He said I should leave fun reading, like the novels and spiritual books he assigned, in the bathroom so I could only read them in there. I laughed at that, but he was really serious. He said if that's what it takes, you do it! So I did.

In spite of my efforts, however, I started to panic as the final exam approached. I spoke to Rama about one week before the dreaded day, and I had never been so worried over an exam in my life. I found myself telling him I was afraid I was going to fail. I had always been a good student, and the thought of failing really bothered me. But he barely let me finish. In a stern and commanding voice he said, "It would be VERY bad karma if you failed this course. Very, very bad!" This definitely got my attention, and I stopped fretting enough to listen to him. He explained that the proper way to prepare for a difficult exam was to study night and day up until the day before without giving up. Then get a good night's rest the night before, no matter how much more studying you think you need. He said seven or eight hours of sleep the night before a test helped more than any last minute studying ever did. There was a hint of laughter in his voice when he said this, as if he remembered those days well!

For the next week I focused completely on studying for my exam. I poured over the material again and again, making sure I understood every concept. If I had to go over something twenty times before I really understood it, I did. Every time I felt panic or I wanted to give up in frustration, I pushed those feelings down with my will and redirected my focus towards the seemingly impossible task of assimilating the material in front of me. The effort paid off; by the last day I knew I had finally grasped the material. I went into the exam room feeling a little nervous, but mostly I felt energized by the intense studying, and I was still riding high from Rama's pep talk the week before. I took that final exam feeling the most relaxed I'd ever felt during an exam, and I ended up with an 'A' in the course. From this experience I learned that I had more ability and tenacity than I thought, and this realization gave me the confidence to take on many subsequent challenges in business and in the personal domain as well.

I am a professional musician who supplements his income by working as a part-time computer programmer. A number of the artists and music producers I work with are quite well known. I attribute most of my artistic, personal, spiritual, and professional growth in the last six years to what I learned during my association with Rama.

In 1992 and 1993, when Rama was touring the country giving lectures on a regular basis, he would hold banquets at upscale hotels in San Francisco for his students and their guests. Those who attended would be treated to a lavish meal in a posh setting, after which Rama would speak and teach meditation. It was during one of these banquets that Rama asked that those of us in the room who aspired to be professional musicians stand up. I stood, as did a few others.

Rama's gaze slowly settled in turn on each would-be musician standing in the dining room. The colors in the room appeared to shift, and everything began to take on a strange gold sheen. The room and everything in it rippled, as if everything I saw was actually a reflection in a pond, and the water was gently stirring. Rama himself was nearly invisible behind the light that seemed to radiate from him. The room vibrated. My body began to shake. When he turned to face me, his eyes captured my attention. They were deep, dark, and unfathomable.

I didn't notice any major change in my musical ability. However, my music teacher did. Every time I came in for a lesson in the six months following that seminar, my music teacher would rave, dumbfounded at the sudden phenomenal improvement in my playing.

One night, three friends and I went to a diner in upper Westchester for a late-night snack. At that time it was not uncommon to see other students of Rama in the area, since one of his businesses was located nearby. We were sitting near the bathrooms. I saw one of Rama's associates walk by to go into the bathroom. It did not even cross my mind that Rama might be there because I was very involved in conversation. But I turned my head and looked clear across the restaurant to a booth where Rama was sitting facing me. The seat which had been occupied by his associate was now empty, giving a clear view. The moment I looked in his direction, I was completely put into a trance. It was as if I went somewhere else for a second - sort of blanked out. Then, all of the sudden as I came out of the trance, I realized that I was staring right at him and he was staring right at me! What was only a few seconds felt to contain so much. I realize that for anyone reading this story who has never been in Rama's presence or that of another Enlightened Being, this could sound strange. It's a rather difficult thing to explain, the feeling that one gets when one is in the presence of an Enlightened Being or getting "zapped" by one, as was definitely the case here. I don't know how, but he has the ability to change a person from the inside out. And you definitely feel it when he does!

The thing that made this experience extra special for me was what he gave me that evening. I'll have to give a tiny bit of background: I am a musician who has played and written music for the majority of my life. It's one of the things that brings me joy. Around that time I was thinking about taking a leap in my musical "career". I was thinking about putting my own band together and being the lead singer. I had been in many bands as a guitarist but thought that being a lead singer was an impossibility, because I believed that I could not sing. There were also some things about my song-writing that I was thinking that I needed to improve.

Well, guess what was the topic of discussion with my friends the night I saw Rama at the restaurant - it was all about starting a band and various discussions surrounding the entire topic.

In the weeks following this encounter I found myself writing songs one after another. I had a surge of songs pouring out of me faster than I ever had before. I would stay up until 2 or 3 a.m., just pouring songs out onto my tape machine. And they were definitely improved in the areas that I felt I needed improvement. Shortly thereafter, I started a band in which I was the singer and played most of the songs I had written during this time. I felt as if I were on a mission.

I am no longer in that particular band, but I am still greatly involved in other musical projects. And I'm still singing! This has caused me to grow, not only as a musician, but as a person because I was able to arrive at a place in my life that, at one time, I had thought was only a silly fantasy. The realization of that dream made me see that there is no end to the possibilities of what a person can achieve. Of course, a little help from Rama certainly doesn't hurt!

I look back on that night as a very special night in my life and I'm very thankful for that gift that he gave me.

After working late one night on a software project, Rama invited a few of us to go over to the local diner for something to eat. As we stepped out of the office building into the balmy and humid New York summer night, Rama turned and asked me if I wanted to ride with him. That question required no deliberation on my part, as I had always wanted to get a ride in Rama's car. He told me to wait while he pulled around. A minute later his black V12 Mercedes pulled to a stop, purring softly and powerfully by the curb. The passenger door opened and I got in.

The first thing I thought, as I sunk into the massive leather seat, was that this wasn't a normal car. A myriad of lights, gauges and communication devices ran all the way across the dashboard, making it look more like the cockpit of an airplane. I had climbed into Rama's "Command and Control" center, not into a passenger vehicle! Rama didn't look at me when he said, "You're only the second person to ride in this car." That made me even more nervous. I sat very still, trying to quiet my mind, as I've learned that a person's thoughts in a physical environment can leave impressions that psychics will sense long after that person physically departs. The last thing I wanted to do was leave my thought "fingerprints" in Rama's car.

But my fears were blasted to bits a moment later when Rama turned on his sound system. There was going to be no conversation on this journey — heavy-metal rock filled the car with a sudden fury as we pulled quickly out of the parking lot. The music wasn't just loud — it was all around me and seemed to be penetrating my bones. The music was so consuming that I forgot about being nervous and just listened. In contrast to the soul-scorching music, Rama drove slowly and carefully as we headed toward the diner.

We sat down to eat, and Rama started playing James Taylor songs on the jukebox. With a total lack of self-consciousness, he sang along with the tunes in his soft and melodious tenor - he knew every word and every note. His voice blended beautifully with James Taylor's, and Rama seemed as innocent as a teenager who memorizes all his favorite songs.

After eating, we got back into the car. Rama put the heavy-metal music back on, full volume. It occurred to me at that moment, that he was not seeing the same things when he drove that I was seeing. I remembered his comment from a lecture years before when he mentioned that while most people see everyday objects in the world as fixed and static objects, he sees the world as energy patterns, as shapes and formations of shifting, living light. Everything is alive, he said, and it's just our conditioning that prevents us from seeing things as they really are. I could only imagine what a challenge it must have been for him to drive!

When we got back to the office, I got out of the car and started towards my own car and my way home. I got into my economy model Honda with its tidy fabric bucket seats and its plastic molded dashboard. I felt very different, of course, like I had stepped out of a five-star restaurant into a Burger King. It became very clear to me at that moment that the environment that we choose to surround ourselves with impacts the type and quality of thoughts that we think. I understood why money is so important to a modern spiritual seeker: we need it in order to establish an environment that will be conducive to the meditative practice, because it's impractical and probably illegal to live in a cave. I thanked Rama inwardly for showing me his "cave". A few months later I leased a luxury car, which had a profound effect on my self-image and my level of inner peace.

Rama walked into the room and sat down. I was busy working on a new computer program.

"How's it going?" he inquired.

I smiled. I had been hoping he would drop by. I handed him a finished piece of CD-ROM software that we had been working on for several years. It was an electronic version of the *I Ching*, the ancient book of Chinese wisdom. We had developed it into an interactive graphics program, complete with text and a section to ask a question and get an answer. We had added a soundtrack using music from Zazen, the electronic music group that Rama produced.

"Here it is." I said.

He took the package and looked it over. "'Bout time. I like the packaging."

"I'm not sure it will run well on your Personal Computer system at home," I began.

"No problem," he said. "It's not necessary."

He looked down at the package, opened it, examined the CD-ROM, and read the liner notes. I started to tell him about some cool features we had added, but he wasn't listening. Slowly the room filled with a beautiful gold light. I felt the world spin away, and I was sitting there in the clearest, sharpest, brightest state of mind I had ever known.

Rama stood up, smiled, and whacked me on the head with the package as he walked out.

It was the spring of 1995, and Rama had called together all of his students for a business meeting and meditation at the State University of New York, Purchase Performing Arts Center. We were in the large theater, usually used for ballets, symphonies and plays. But on this particular evening there were scheduled presentations of software business plans by three or four of Rama's students.

Rama had asked me to present a business plan for the company that he and I had started together one year before. We had finished the development of our initial prototype product and it was time to bring more people into the company to assist with the development of our version 1 release. I was really nervous, as I had never stood up in front of so many people before. There were at least four hundred people in attendance.

I decided to try and present our software by flipping back and forth between a software demonstration and a series of PowerPoint slides. As I got into the presentation, I realized that the time it was taking to flip back and forth was unacceptable. While I hadn't found my computer to be particularly slow when I had practiced the presentation, now, in front of hundreds of expectant eyes, it was unbearable.

To make up for the time spent watching the Microsoft Windows hourglass symbol hang on the screen, I began talking extemporaneously about the software. I felt my voice rising and didn't really know exactly what I was saying. I also found myself walking furiously around the stage, in the hope that my movements would distract the audience from the stuttering visual presentation.

About five minutes into this chaotic talk, Rama suddenly walked up onto the stage. He approached me and gently asked for the microphone. Rama said, "He is not explaining this product properly. So I'm going to do the presentation for him." Though I was surprised, I also felt flattered that he had felt so strongly about the product to have come up on the stage and taken control of the presentation.

I walked off the stage and down into the aisle by the orchestra pit, next to the first row of seats. All seats were filled, so I stood there in the shadows while Rama calmly and clearly described our product in considerable detail. He finished in about ten minutes. While I felt humbled, I also felt good. Rama then called the next presenter onto the stage, handed over the microphone, and walked off the stage. He approached me, and as the next presentation began, told me to sit down.

I looked around, a little confused, because all the seats were filled. "Sit down right here," he whispered, so I promptly sat down cross-legged on the carpeted aisle next to the first row. I looked up at the stage where the next presentation was underway. To my surprise, Rama sat down right next to me, on my right side, and wrapped his long arm around my shoulder. I felt like a young football player being encouraged by his coach after blowing an easy touchdown.

Rama leaned over and whispered in my ear, "Watch her. She's very good at what she does." He gestured with his gaze at the woman presenting her company's product. As I watched her I noticed that the crowd seemed entranced by her easy cadence, her relaxed posture, and her elegant attire. Rama said, "She has everyone's complete attention. This is what you need to learn how to do. Watch!" I continued to watch, and at the same time was very conscious of Rama's closeness, as he had never actually put his arm around me before.

Rama stayed there, sitting on the carpet in his expensive suit with his arm around me for about five minutes, and then stood up and moved away. I stayed there, watching the rest of the presentation and thinking about how everyone probably thought that I felt terrible and embarrassed. Actually I felt absolutely great, electrified and at the same time humbled. Most importantly, I felt I had learned something about myself, and I vowed to learn how to make really good business presentations.

As it turned out, since that day I have made over 500 business presentations to groups all over the world, and have been a featured speaker at major computer-industry conferences. I have Rama to thank for showing me my shortcomings and giving me the insight and encouragement to improve myself.

People have some really weird ideas about Rama's program. One of the more ridiculous assertions is that Rama's students are weak people who were somehow persuaded to give

Rama lots of money for something totally intangible. They have obviously never met any of us, nor do they have any idea what was really involved in his program for career success. The people who actually worked with him on a long-term basis find this accusation rather mystifying because they are highly intelligent, ambitious, hard-working, career-minded individuals who have a real interest in promoting themselves financially as well as spiritually, and have had to overcome a great deal of personal history, pain and opposition to do it.

The bottom line is that in our culture, what gives you freedom is financial independence. My own career success, most definitely a result of Rama's program, is a real example of unparalleled gains of an investment that I, reasonably, must consider the best I ever made, since it brought me financial independence.

I met Rama in the spring of 1992, at the end of my junior year in college. In addition to inspiring me, by the witness of countless miracles, to start meditating on a regular basis, I became very intrigued by the software program he had set up for his older students. I had expected to see a lot of "New Age" types at the meetings he held, but was instead surprised to see professional, together-looking people in nice business suits with an obvious air of financial success. I was particularly interested in seeing very successful businesswomen there. They seemed self-assured and had a certain level of sophistication that I found very interesting.

At the time, I had no real career plans. In fact, I would say that I didn't have a very strong sense of what Rama called the "really real world" was like at all. Over the next year, while finishing up my liberal arts degree requirements, I enrolled also in a couple of computer programming courses to give it a try.

Surprisingly, although I found them difficult, I really enjoyed the mental challenge of struggling with logical constructs and syntactical precision. I remember doing little victory dances in my room at 3:00 in the morning, from time to time, after finally getting a tricky piece of code to compile and run successfully.

After I graduated in 1993, admittedly, I didn't really have any marketable job skills. Although I had always been considered very intelligent, academically successful, and ambitious, I didn't really have a sense of a specific direction in which to head. My first job out of college was as a receptionist for $10 per hour. However, I remained hopeful about the possibilities of a software career. I just didn't know how I was going to do it. That fall, Rama escalated the program for his newer students. Over the next year and a half or so, I tried to learn as much as I could about software and I took a few chances, moving to New York where he was centering more advanced software courses.

After a few interim steps in which I was dealing with a lot of internal struggles about my own belief in my ability to learn technical skills, I landed my first real programming job at the end of 1994. Rama had offered some excellent, practical courses, which were taught by software professionals working in the industry. While, technically, the courses were certainly outstanding, what made it possible to learn so quickly was the empowerment and encouragement Rama gave his students on a regular basis.

Eventually, I landed my first programming job, which paid $35,000 per year. Once I saw that I could really do the work, I became hungry to learn more and more. Over the next few years, Rama set up additional courses, to which I really applied myself. The energy I was gaining from meditation and from Rama directly acted as a catalyst, allowing me to make jumps that most people would never think possible. Not only was I becoming more technically knowledgeable, but also my mind was "growing" for lack of a better way to explain it. I could just "get" things very quickly.

In 1995, I got my first software contract position which paid $35 an hour. The jumps kept occurring until, in four years, I had made income increases of over 800%! This is not normal. Some people might think that it is ridiculous, that somehow I "tricked" people in to thinking I knew more than I did, but this is just not the case. I am worth every penny of it. I can now create information systems which improve business, increase profits, and create greater efficiencies.

Software and coding is not something you can fool people into thinking you know. Either you can do the job or you can't. It's pretty obvious. In working with Fortune 500 companies, managers recognized my technical and problem-solving abilities and what several of them described as an "intangible" quality, or would describe me as "very bright". Their seeing me this way was undoubtedly the power of Rama's energy shining through me, which he constantly gave his students in order to make this kind of rapid progress (both financial and spiritual) possible. While certainly a great deal of this success can be attributed to gains in my sense of self-esteem and confidence, and my own technical and intellectual abilities and ambition, I have no doubt that without Rama's constant guidance, support, encouragement, and empowerment, this would not have been possible.

Some people seem to have a problem with Rama's focus on financial and career success. The money itself has never been the point. It is just a measuring stick by which to judge that something else is working, something invisible. While certainly the spiritual side of things is really "the point" and what creates a sense of happiness and balance, it is very difficult to objectively measure "spiritual progress".

Rama used to compare this enigma to the wind, saying, "You can't see the wind, but you can see the leaves on the trees moving. That is how you know the wind is blowing." Career and financial success are the leaves, moving, the outer manifestation of the power, wisdom, insight, and strength gained through spiritual practice. Some part of us needs to see, and feel, real and tangible progress, to see that our efforts are paying off.

What I invested in the software courses and other aspects of the "life success program" over the last four years was much less than I spent on my University education (which could not even come close to providing the depth and practicality I needed for the real world). Just doing the math should prove to even the most cynical critic, that there was something very beneficial about Rama's program. I do consider it, personally, my best financial investment.

Prior to meeting Rama in the 1980's I had been employed in the data processing industry for over fourteen years and had worked my way up through the application development ranks to the position of senior project manager for a national department store chain. Many of Rama's students at that time were unskilled and took odd jobs with no consideration or thought given to career advancement. After attending Rama's meditation classes for a while, I noticed that he often suggested to his students that they consider computer science as a career. This somehow seemed to go against the grain of the New Age community at the time, for most people drawn to meditation in this country seemed to have the idea that spiritual progress, balance, and wisdom were to be obtained by withdrawing from the world. Rama was teaching that these things were obtained, not by running away, but by going into the world and doing everything perfectly with total focus and attention to detail.

Rama's interest in computer science grew rapidly. He put together a computer-oriented career advancement seminar for his students which started with teaching data entry and word processing, and that later stepped up to computer programming in COBOL and C. As many of his students became proficient in programming, he started giving a series of classes that taught everyone beginning and advanced relational databases. After many students mastered relational databases he proceeded to give classes in mathematics, artificial intelligence and in software product development.

Rama's emphasis on career success mixed with meditation and Buddhist empowerments produced *phenomenal* results. Over the years I have seen hundreds of people rapidly advance their careers using this template. What I noticed most in this process is that whenever someone made an advancement in their career, they would simultaneously make a quantum leap in their self-confidence, maturity, and sophistication. The inner and outer worlds reflect one another. Rama said the primary reason people do not continue to advance in their careers is *fear* and that the second biggest reason is *laziness*. Whenever I have made career advances it was because I won a battle in the war against these two opponents, and with each win the quality and depth of my daily meditations would significantly increase.

When Rama first started giving computer career classes, I felt an affinity for his point of view, however I did not personally involve myself in this educational program. I had been in the industry for fourteen years and was working as the lead database administrator for an international hotel chain. I assumed that I knew everything there was to know about computer science.

It was then that I started noticing something strange about Rama's students. These young "kids" with only two or three years experience were starting to display a depth of knowledge and experience in a number of computer-related fields that surpassed my own, even in my area of specialization which was relational databases. By taking Rama's computer classes and by following his meditation and focusing techniques, these "kids" were able to do in two to three years what it took me fifteen years to do. Suddenly I realized that I was being left behind!

That is when I decided to start taking Rama's computer classes.

The programming and relational database classes were not taught by academics, but rather were taught by people currently working in the field, many of whom were also students of Rama. Rama insisted that these classes be stripped of all unnecessary frills and that focus be placed totally upon learning that which the employer needed.

After some of my experiences in college, it was refreshing to see someone actually coordinating classroom content to the real needs of industry.

During my early years studying with Rama, I related to him primarily as a meditation teacher (and later as a martial arts teacher). I did not, however, view him as a computer science teacher. This illusion was utterly demolished one day when I had the opportunity to sit in on a product design session with Rama and some of his students who had advanced degrees in computer science and math. Rama talked and they listened. Rama was describing how to build a sophisticated software product that involved an unusual hybrid of neural networks, self-learning expert systems, and genetic algorithms. As we say in computer lingo, his audience was "paging heavily".

It was then that I first realized that Rama had an intimate knowledge of the most sophisticated computer technologies on the planet. After making considerable progress myself, I was able to attend the classes on product design and applications of artificial intelligence to business and military problems that were taught by Rama himself. With thirty years of computer experience now under my belt, not once have I ever met anyone that showed the level of genius Rama displayed in the world of software design.

In the early 90's, Rama started providing business seminars for his students. These classes were designed to teach people how to start their own businesses and create and market their own software products. Rama taught these classes personally.

His emphasized the importance of going out and interviewing many people in our target markets to identify what it is that they needed and wanted. We would actually go to trade shows with no product, and rather than selling, we would ask people what it is that they want. This was received quite warmly. Trade show attendees seem to appreciate the fact that someone really cared about their business needs.

Once we completed the first version of a product, we then would go back to the trade shows. Again we were primarily seeking feedback for improvement rather than trying to sell. If the product seemed on track, we would then deliver the product to a few "beta sites" to get more detailed client feedback. This usually sent us back to the drawing board with several design changes. At this point we would have a viable software product.

For those that succeeded at creating a marketable software product, Rama had advanced seminars teaching them how to do marketing and set up distribution networks. If this succeeded, he then showed his students how to position for and either sell or take the company public. His knowledge of the dynamics of American business never ceased to amaze me.

The response by his students to this business program varied. Some chose not to be involved in this module of his program. Some made halfhearted attempts, and some threw themselves into it with their total being. The students that were most successful were the ones that were able to best conquer their own *fears* and overcome their own *laziness*. As of this writing, several students have sold companies at considerable profit. One of these sales was to a premier software company that has made dozens of aggressive acquisitions. The company Rama's students sold to them has turned out to be the parent company's *most profitable acquisition to-date.*

Some people are unable to reconcile spiritualism with fighting. Rama taught that fighting for what is the Dharma (essential correctness) creates rapid spiritual growth and that many (but not all) people that claim to be pacifists have simply not overcome their fears.

Some people are unable to reconcile spiritualism with a strong self-image and successful careers. Rama's perspective was that to survive the rigors of advanced meditative practice an extremely strong mind is required. Succeeding at a career, particularly in computer science, requires development of analytical abilities and overcoming of fears that map directly to the skills needed for traversing advanced meditative states. Having a career has an additional advantage in that not all of your personal energy need be deployed towards daily physical survival, leaving some energy for pursuit of self-discovery.

Some people are unable to reconcile spiritualism with money. Just like kundalini energy, money is a form of power. It can be used to make things happen. In and of itself it is neither good nor bad; however, the hand that wields it can definitely direct it towards light or darkness. Considerable balance and strength of heart and mind is required to not be corrupted by power. However, to have a strong heart and mind and to have no power at your command is the fast path to becoming a victim in today's abrasive world.

I realize now that if many years ago Rama had not spent over $100,000 to produce a particular public meditation seminar series, I would have never met him.

I think about that quite often.

Desert Trips

Rama had a great love for the deserts of the American Southwest and took his students there many times during the 1980's and early 1990's. One day in my first year of study he announced that he would be conducting a "desert trip". I was taken aback by how extraordinarily attentive everyone in the audience became. He proceeded to explain, for the benefit of the newer students present, that a desert trip was an opportunity to make a quantum leap in one's personal power through direct experiential contact with the higher Occult, and said that a fundamental reordering of one's sense of reality would occur if the trip was handled properly. He said that we would be traveling at night on foot through desert regions where the doorways to other dimensional planes were more easily accessed, and that the energy in these locations was similar in many aspects to the energies in Tibet. He indicated that a desert trip was not to be taken lightly, and that we should prepare for it as if we were preparing for a martial arts tournament - we should have tightened up all aspects of our lives and should be in peak physical, mental, and emotional condition upon arrival. He then proceeded to say something I took at that time to be a joke. He said that we should all clean out our closets at home before leaving, and that we should do it as a polite gesture to the person who would be returning. After my first trip into the desert with Rama, I realized that this was no joke.

One month later I found myself driving through the Anza Borego desert of Southern California. About ten miles from our rendezvous point I started visually scanning for where I thought I was going to end up. I could see in all directions for approximately thirty miles. The sky was completely overcast in all directions as there was not a single break in the cloud cover anywhere. Then I noticed an exception. Right where I thought I was headed was a gaping hole in the cloud cover that must have been two or three thousand feet in diameter. This alone would not have aroused my suspicion, however floating in the middle of this "clearing" were two very precisely defined clouds. One was in the shape of a doughnut (without the hole in the middle), several hundred feet in diameter. The other was in the shape of a giant apostrophe - it looked like a big finger pointing at the ground. As I got closer I discovered that, sure enough, the big finger was pointing directly at my destination. It occurred to me that the only thing larger than Rama's love for his students was the outrageousness of his sense of humor.

After parking my car, I took a brief walk up a riverbed and joined other students who had arrived before me. As the sun set behind the mountains we sat quietly and meditated. Sometime after dark Rama arrived and proceeded to give us instructions on how to travel with him safely through the desert in total darkness. As he was talking, a most unusual wind started blowing out of the west. It very steadily and evenly increased from being barely noticeable until it was blowing at forty or fifty miles per hour, making it difficult for us to focus on the instructions being given. Rama's elegant figure was silhouetted against the starlit horizon. In a clear and confident voice he was telling us that, as students, we should not go into isolated areas of the desert at night by ourselves. He said that because of the energy he had "loaned" us, our auras were exceptionally bright and this could attract maleficent forces that would otherwise not bother with us. We continued to get sandblasted as the wind steadily increased in velocity. I was no longer listening to our teacher. It was occurring to me that we were rapidly approaching a point where I would have to lay down and grab hold of a rock to prevent my being, quite literally, blown away. I had to cover my eyes to protect them from the sand. The wind continued to increase.

Three things then happened simultaneously: (1) I inwardly lost my calm and started to be overcome by an unusual panic, (2) Rama yelled quite loudly, "Enough already!!" and (3) the wind instantly stopped — totally and completely stopped. I stumbled awkwardly trying not to fall over. I was astounded! Here I was standing in a desert filled with perfectly calm air, and was watching sand fall out of the sky in little swirls. Rama calmly continued his discourse as if nothing had happened, and later we started our nighttime adventure into the magical desert about us. Not a word was said about our encounter with the wind.

After a rather aggressive hike in total darkness, we stopped in an area surrounded on three sides by hills. He asked us to sit and focus our attention on a very bright star that had just risen from behind the mountain that we were facing. I had noticed it earlier. It was a planet and was by far the brightest object visible at that time. Since the afternoon, the sky had cleared in all directions, and I could no longer detect clouds anywhere. I focused on the star and worked on trying to stop my thoughts. After two or three minutes, I noticed the star slightly flicker. Something was happening to it. Then it went out. Completely out. Black. Not there. My shock was so great that I found myself laying on my back on the ground - I must have fallen over from a sitting position. A giant "Ooooohhhhh" emanated from the group. The star popped back in and once again dominated the sky, bright as ever. Over the following five-minute period, this star-on, star-off process repeated itself several times, destroying any remnant of disbelief arising in my mind. At some point something in me snapped and I realized what he was doing. He was manifesting and dispersing a small opaque cloud between us and the star. While this was no less miraculous, it somehow made it easier for the rational part of my mind to accept the experience.

After a "bathroom break" we proceeded to walk farther up the riverbed that we were following. Hiking seemed easier. I could now see much better in the dark, and my feet felt like they were barely touching the ground, which now looked more like luminous snow than sand. When we stopped next, it was difficult for me to assess how far we had traveled — my ability to track time seemed somehow impaired. However, from my sweat-soaked clothes I gathered that we must have walked quite far. Rama had us sit about him in a semicircle and explained that he was going to open a doorway to another dimension. I sat upright and was able to quiet down my thoughts more than I usually could when meditating. I could feel him shifting us quickly through many levels of attention. As I sat there watching him, I noticed a spot appear in the air above him and slightly to his left. A circular area of "wavy" air was forming that was about ten feet in diameter. It looked just like something from Star Trek that was "cloaked" by a Klingon cloaking device. Very fine fibers of white light then proceeded to emerge from the circular area and began coalescing into a form. The image of a giant white bird with a thirty-foot wingspan, constructed completely of luminous white fibers, appeared before us. It was quite exquisite.

Afterwards Rama asked students to describe what they had experienced. Many different other things were reported which I did not see. One person then described the bird. Rama seemed quite interested in this and asked how many people saw it. It sounded as if over half of the group had seen it. Rama told us that this is his form in another dimensional plane. I had the distinct impression that a most positive omen had just occurred.

Rama then again had us stop our thoughts and watch him. It became extraordinarily quiet. Two things started happening at the same time. Rama and a rectangular area about him started becoming darker and darker, and everything else became brighter and brighter. There was incredible intensity in simply being alive, sitting there, and observing what was happening. This continued until Rama was transformed into a large black rectangle eight feet tall and four feet wide. However, the desert around us was bright as midday. At this point, four beams of brilliant light emanated from the black rectangle and radiated in four directions. It was a very intense experience. I have absolutely no sense of how long this process lasted.

At the end of our walk back out of the desert, we stood in a large circle. Rama stood at the center. I noticed that occasional flashes of light would emanate from his feet and would zig-zag about on the ground. It looked like little bolts of lightning. He then proceeded to touch each of us on our third eye. He said that tonight had been a very important night for all of us. My body agreed.

Upon returning home, I found my relationship with this world to be irrevocably altered. Things that previously would have irritated or annoyed me seemed inconsequential. The underlying motivations of people around me became more transparent. My abilities in computer science made a quantum leap. I was able to hold multiple complex and highly interrelated concepts in my mind at once in ways I never could before. My meditations became more fun and more consistent. My desire to introduce others to the magical world of self-discovery increased, and my capacity to see humor in the most ridiculous of situations greatly expanded. And I did truly appreciate my former self for having the courtesy to clean and organize my closet in preparation for my return.

Miracles and psychic phenomena were always a given around Rama. However, some people tended to "see" more than others, either because they were more developed psychically or just less blocked up. Although I was one of those people who usually didn't see a lot of psychic phenomena, I did have several memorable experiences during one of our trips to the desert.

It was near midnight on the night before the summer solstice, and we were all seated in the sand around Rama. I think it was one of the largest groups he had ever brought out to the desert. It was often hard to hear what he was saying because he moved to different parts of the circle as he talked and gave his performance. At one point, while he was talking animatedly about something, a white, phosphorescent light appeared in the area around his feet. It looked like he had waded into a shallow pool of something like wispy, white cotton candy. Suddenly he was doing Michael Jackson's moonwalk – on top of the light, about six inches off of the ground! Then the light formed a short staircase, about five or six feet high, and he ran up and down it a few times. Then the light wrapped itself around his legs, pulling on him in a gentle tug-of-war as he tried to walk. As he pulled unsuccessfully against the playful white tendrils, I heard him say, "Sometimes, the light just grabs onto you...and no matter what you do, it just won't let go! See what I mean?" and, laughing like a child, he grabbed his own leg and pulled on it for emphasis. Later, he completely disappeared; first his head, then his body seemed to evaporate into the air, so I could see the stars and the landscape clearly, right through the area where he had just been standing. This kind of thing went on for hours every night.

Experiences like this one have taught me that the physical world isn't exactly as it seems. This realization has evoked in me a deep respect for the mysteries of life. It has also taught me to let go of some of the smaller annoyances and negative feelings that I experience, since all of that is pretty insignificant in the face of the kind of phenomena and magic we all witnessed as Rama's students. It also showed me that I shouldn't take myself too seriously, either, since I'm obviously very insignificant in the face of that powerful and mysterious side of life, and it made me feel grateful for witnessing some truly beautiful, unusual and magical moments. At the same time it showed me that I was a part of all that timeless mystery, too. Perhaps most importantly, however, these experiences made me aware of the unrealized potential that existed in me. They showed me there were greater possibilities in life than I had ever dreamed of. They gave me the impetus to break down the barriers between who I am and who I want to be, whether that involves becoming a successful businesswoman, a respected technologist, a black belt in martial arts, or a person who is really, truly at peace.

I don't remember how the conversation started, but here's the scene:

It was a spring equinox trip in the desert, around 1992. On the third night of our four-night trip, it was raining cats and dogs, so Rama decided that we would spend the evening in the living room of someone's rented house. About thirty of us were sitting around in the living room. I had arrived early that night and had picked a seat that I thought would be close to

Rama. I got lucky, and Rama sat about seven feet from where I was, with no one between us. The feeling was very intimate in the room.

Rama's kundalini was really strong that night, and I could feel its heat and pressure, cooking me away. At some point, I asked a question. Rama turned his attention to me and started teasing me a little. Then he got serious and said, "You know, you really need to clear that energy out of your navel area or you're going to get sick. You could die of dysentery, you know." A sly and subtle grin crossed his face. A few of us laughed at this statement. "Dysentery is a terrible way to die!" he continued in a serious and concerned tone.

Rama then proceeded onto an extended monologue about flatulence and the misfortune of death by dysentery. He talked in great detail about the noise, the mess, and the stench of dysentery, not to mention the inconvenience. Most of us were laughing pretty hard, and some people were really losing it. I was doubled over, unable to control myself, occasionally screaming with joy. Rama described almost all of this in a completely deadpan tone with just a sparkle in his eye and a slight grin on his face. Every now and then, though, he had to laugh too. It was just too funny.

A few times he stopped talking about it, let the laughter subside, and went on to answer someone else's question. But the discussion would always turn back to dysentery. He would throw a word like "explode" into his conversation with someone, then look my way, and we would start laughing all over again. This went on for thirty minutes, maybe longer. Eventually I felt I couldn't laugh any more. He'd exhausted the topic, and we were exhausted too. I was collapsed on the floor. My eyes had been streaming tears. My stomach ached so much from laughing that part of me wanted him to stop making jokes. But Rama wouldn't quit; he just kept coming up with more things to say.

Finally we thought it was over. He was talking about the moment of death. "You'll be lying in a hospital bed somewhere, barely breathing. Your apprentices will be gathered around you. 'Oh, she was so good to us!' they'll say. And then..." his voice trailed off and he paused dramatically and silently, "one last fart!" That was it. No one could withstand the mirth. The room was roaring with laughter. We were being transmuted. Rama was laughing, too. That was a good night!

On a desert trip one summer Rama gave me a gift. I was already a veteran of several desert trips. I was starting to get used to them in the sense that they weren't so awesome and mind-blowing, and I was taking them for granted. These feelings were reinforced when the first half of the desert trip almost completely matched my expectations. On the second half of the trip, Rama snapped me out of my complacency.

He told us to lie on our backs and watch the sky. Normally, he would tell us what he was about to do and then do it, but this time he said to just be still and watch. Since I had no idea what he was about to do, and experience had taught me he could pull off the most outrageous things, I got myself into a high state of alertness and kept myself ready for anything.

After about twenty seconds, the constellations began to shift around and change. The stars rearranged themselves into different patterns, and I became aware that I was looking into different skies. This happened to me on nearly every desert trip, and I was certain it was going to go down the same way this time. However, because Rama hadn't said what he was going to do, I kept paying attention.

At one point, I noticed a line of light in the sky. At first I thought a meteor had hit the atmosphere and left a trail, but the line remained. It went straight across the sky, rather than in an arc. After about ten seconds, it was still there, and it was the only thing different about what I was seeing, so I focused on it. I sensed it had intelligence. As I focused on it, two more lines appeared. After a few seconds of wondering what they were, I focused on them and more appeared. This kept going on for a while, and each time more lines appeared, a pressure in my solar plexus grew.

At one point, when there were thirty-three lines in the sky, criss-crossing each other, my perception changed. I knew that it wasn't that the lines had intelligence; they were intelligence, intelligent awareness. At my realization, the pressure on my navel center increased tremendously, and the lines started whizzing back and forth, and more and more lines began appearing in the sky. Just as the thought crossed my mind to wonder what exactly I was seeing, Rama said to me inwardly, "The lines of the world."

At that, the lines filled the night sky until they completely blocked my view of the stars. They whizzed and vibrated, and just when I felt I couldn't take any more pressure on my navel center, the lines each expanded and then merged into one huge, bright light, brighter than ten thousand suns. I closed my eyes because of the brilliance, but it made no difference. I could still see the light. Then I felt the pressure on my navel center blow me past my boundaries and expand me outward in every direction.

The next thing I remember, we were all walking out of the Gorge, and the sky was starting to get brighter because the dawn was coming. I felt completely cleansed, inside and out. I was light as a feather, and walking was effortless. And I had absolutely no thoughts.

No thoughts at all.

The first desert trip we took was for the summer solstice. The night was cool, and we sat in a semicircle around Rama. The feeling of being out in the desert with him can only be described as magical. Rama asked us to lay back and look at the sky. It was beautiful, clear and full of stars. Then, very subtly yet very definitely, the pattern of stars changed, completely. Then, again they changed. And again, and again. One moment the sky was almost white with so many stars, the next moment it was dark except for a few very bright stars scattered about. With each change, not only the stars would be different, but the feeling and quality of the air also changed. The most extraordinary thing, I realized later, was that at the time there was nothing extraordinary about it. I was in such a wonderfully high meditative state of mind that miracles happened, naturally!

It was New Year's Day 1990, and we were back in the desert after an absence of about three years. We were back to celebrate the New Year with our old friend, the desert.

We met at sunset at our usual power spot. We walked into the desert, and we all sat in a semicircle around Rama. The energy that night was incredible. Rama said that he was going to throw us into the unknown in a way that he had never done before. It was like a certain part of us was never going to come back or be the same again. Rama had reached a new level of power, and he was going to elevate our consciousness in a way not previously experienced.

We meditated for a while, and then he asked us to look up in the sky. He said, "You are now seeing the sky through the eyes of an Enlightened Being." The sky looked more clear than I had ever seen it before. There were thousands of stars in the sky, shining and looking alive. A few of them ran across the sky like shooting stars. The sky was beautiful, and we were one with the sky.

After the meditation was over, we took a break and ate our cold sandwiches, M&M's, and drank our diet cokes. After the break, Rama talked some more about the fact that he was taking us deeper into the Unknown.

Rama said, "I'm going to throw you so deep into the unknown that some of you might not make it back. I'm going to throw all of you into the Unknown, like it was the ocean, and in order for you to come back, you are going to have to swim back to our next seminar one month from now. Some of you might drown in the process, and some others will go in a different direction. If you do, it's okay. If you don't come back, your self-discovery is taking you in different direction, and your soul is choosing to grow at a different rate." Then we meditated again, walked back to our cars, and drove back to our hotels.

The next day I woke up late, took a shower, meditated and went out for lunch. It was such a beautiful day, and I was just happy to be alive. I drove around the desert looking at the big clouds in the sky. I was very grateful to the Universe for giving me such a wonderful opportunity to be there.

In the afternoon we met with Rama at our power spot again. We walked into the desert and sat in front of him. Rama asked us how we felt that day. Some people felt sick, others felt very high. Rama said that whatever we were feeling that day was a reflection of our state of mind. If we felt sick, we should really look into our lives and find out what was making us sick.

Rama said, "1990 is going to give us the opportunity to restructure our lives. We have received this wonderful opportunity called the nineties; we can redo everything that we have done wrong in the past. This is our chance."

We meditated for a long time after Rama spoke to us. It was getting really cold outside, and some dark clouds were coming closer to us. Rama said, "The dark clouds are coming! It's funny how something always wants to keep us away from here, but don't worry, nothing is going to happen."

Rama became very serious and continued by saying, "Do you want to learn a secret?" He said, "I'll tell you the secret of how to not get cold on our desert trips. It's very simple. It's called ski pants." Everybody started laughing. "Yes, you keep some ski pants with you and if it gets cold you put them on. If you are hot you take them off. It's as simple as that." I wished I had thought of it: I was freezing.

The dark clouds were getting closer and darker. Rama decided that we should start walking back towards the road. We would have our final meditation out there instead. We walked back, and then we stopped and formed a circle around him. "Now it is time," Rama said. "I am going to throw you into the Unknown, and I hope to see most of you back in one month. If you don't come back, let me know where you are. Tonight I am restructuring every one of you."

Rama started moving around making martial arts moves, like he was performing a kata. His moves were very graceful, and I felt like I was watching an ancient ceremonial dance. The energy around us became very intense, and bright flashes of energy appeared around his body. Then, the most beautiful event took place. A beam of light came down from the sky, barely visible, and a beautiful bird appeared in front of Rama's heart. He extended his hands, and the bird was moving its violet wings in front of Rama's heart. The bird was shining with violet and purple light. This was no ordinary bird. It was a bird made of pure energy. Then the bird gently disappeared into the sky.

"It is done. I'll see you in a month. Good night." The whole group was very quiet and we started walking back towards the road. My friend came close to me and said, "Well, that was an easy desert trip."

"What are you talking about?" I said, "That was one of the heaviest experiences I've ever had."

She smiled and said, "Oh come on, let's walk faster."

"Okay, I'll race you to the end." When we reached our cars, we said good-bye to the desert. I had changed so much in a couple of days I could not believe it.

A few days after coming back to Los Angeles, I felt really out of place. I started having a lot of problems at work; I just didn't fit in with my normal friends anymore. After two months, I decided to quit my job at the movie studio and I started a new adventure. I wanted to change my career, and I decided to go to computer school. I had already graduated from college, but now I wanted to get into computer programming instead. That trip initiated me into the wonderful world of computer science.

One of my last trips to the desert with Rama was one of the most interesting. A group of about twenty of us had hiked with Rama into the gorge. We sat in a semicircle around him. He stood about twenty feet away from us. Countless small incandescent shapes began to appear in the place where he stood. The shapes floated out of the ground and up into the air, as though they were bubbles coming out of a bubble machine. The shapes were familiar. Some looked like the astrological symbols, others looked like letters of the Greek alphabet, others looked like Egyptian hieroglyphs, and others looked like numbers. Soon I could not see Rama; all I could see were the incredible symbols. As I studied them, I noticed that they were not static. Each symbol constantly transformed itself into some other symbol as it floated up into the sky.

After a while, the shapes began to disappear and I heard Rama's voice, "What's going on out there? What do you see?" One by one, people in the group began describing their experiences. The first few people described scenes that were nothing at all like what I had seen. Then someone began to describe the symbols. Rama said, "Okay, let's see. How do I explain this? What you saw, that's like the factory where the universe is created."

Rama took us on a magical journey to the Anza Borrego desert. Seated in a circle around Rama, we asked him questions and watched him perform miracles of light with his power. He wore a bright yellow running suit, so it was difficult to see where his running suit stopped and his magnificent golden aura began. Rama spoke to us about balance, while balancing with one foot on a rock in the center of our circle.

He said, "In this incarnation you have to have attitude. You have to make a stance. Attitude is a fine line to ego. You have to find it for yourself. Attitude is not being egocentric. It's having a sense of self-worth. It's balance, self-confidence, and feeling good about yourself, but not having an out-of-control ego. You need it to survive, but it can take you out. When you can stand in the middle of things and not be swayed by criticism or praise, that's balance, that's attitude!

"I am the axis of the circle that we form and all the worlds pivot around me. With every movement the worlds are in perfect balance and I hold them in my awareness field. I am the universe. The universe is at my command and the universe commands me. I am all the worlds of light and extreme beauty. I am the worlds of darkness, too, but I live in the worlds of light through my will.

"My job is to proclaim Enlightenment. I stand in the center of all things and say, 'Hi! Here I am. I am Enlightenment.' I am undaunted by praise or criticism. I am perfectly balanced. It's not easy. Try it and see how fast you buckle!"

Rama jumped off of the rock and stood before us in silence as the crescent moon fell behind the mountain. Then he disappeared, and only light remained where we had seen him a moment before. It seemed as if the desert was holding one great breath and didn't dare to let it out while in the presence of such a great Master. While the moon had slipped away, I was sure the sun had come out because the desert floor and the sky were lit with bright golden light. A gentle breeze suddenly made its way down the gorge as Rama spoke to end the evening.

"I am the center. I am the core of a mandala that we create as part of a Buddhist collective. As a group, we form and are the life of the mandala. The matrix of the lines of light of the desert floor, which extends from me to each of you, creates a beautiful mandala of light - a visual mandala of our strength as a group striving for the center of Enlightenment, the worlds of endless light and beauty beyond comprehension."

Fun

About five years ago, we as a group were working on getting our first computer job. However, my highest priority was…funniness.

At Rama's seminars, he was always telling jokes and making us laugh. I could not understand half of his jokes since I did not grow up in America, and most of the jokes were heavily based on American culture. I found myself laughing with the crowd without really knowing what was going on. I was quite distressed that I was not funny enough.

I went home and meditated on how to be funny. After one month of meditating on the subject, I decided to ask Rama about how to be funny, since he was the funniest person I have ever met.

During the break at one of the seminars, I took all my courage and went up to my teacher. We bowed and said hi to each other. I said to him, "Can you teach me how to be funny?" In my mind, I pictured that he would assign me a list of funny books to read, and I was ready to write down the recommended list.

He looked at me and said, "You are the first person to ask me this question, after years of teaching meditation. Very good. I will put you on the path. I will teach you telepathically." I found myself talking to my own mind, "Is there a path of funniness? You mean I do not need to do computer science? What do you mean by you will be teaching me telepathically?" I was a bit puzzled, but I thanked him very much. We bowed, and he started to walk away. Then he turned around and said to me again, "After all, we all decide to be funny."

Following that seminar, I woke up during the middle of night and sat up laughing hysterically, then went back to sleep. This happened about three nights in a row.

Since that time, humor and laughter have transformed my life. For example, when I teach meditation there is always a tremendous amount of laughter in the classroom. Jokes come at just the right moment. Some people actually show up for my classes because they see the word "laughter" in the class advertisement. Comedies are my favorite films. I can understand more jokes now. I try to make fun of myself constantly. When I laugh, it rekindles my bond with Rama.

Our second rave with Rama was at the Puck Building in New York City. At raves with Rama, we danced for hours and hours without tiring. Rama raised our consciousness to the point that our minds were completely silent. We didn't even notice that we had entered a meditative state, because he made it seem so natural. Sometimes, I saw Rama walk up to some unsuspecting person and ask them what they were thinking. Every time, the person replied that although they had not noticed before, they were in a state of meditation, without thoughts.

At this rave, I took a moment to notice my state of mind. Normally, my mind would have been full of thoughts from my day and all of the things going on in my life, but that night was different. Thoughts came into my mind and vanished just as quickly. I knew that Rama was keeping us in a perfect state of meditation as we danced. I felt freedom that I had never felt before. I was completely free to dance. I realized that dancing was just another form of meditation for Rama. Rama always said that dancing is the movement of life.

I woke up after seven hours of sleep on Nevis feeling completely refreshed and rested, wondering how that was possible given that it took me 40 hours of travel with no sleep to get there, and I hadn't slept much for several days before leaving.

The next night, after our meeting with Rama, I was in my room and found myself drawn to opening my door. Rama was approaching my room! He came over and casually leaned on the doorjamb. I knew he was trying to make me feel comfortable by being so casual, but I was beside myself anyway. We had a conversation in the doorway, which for me consisted of trying to understand what felt like a thousand unspoken words for every one he spoke out loud. He told me that I was in a very good location aurically, since he was staying directly above my room! This was an awesome thing to find out. When he said goodnight and went upstairs, I immediately split for the beach to try to get a grip, and get my attention totally clean before returning to the room to try to go to sleep. I now understood why I had awakened so refreshed that morning!

On the third night, after the meeting, which was comedy night, I went out on the beach to sit for a while. The evening had been really high, and the room had been infused with gold light. The meeting started in complete silence. Rama was sitting on the stage, eyes closed, with no music on. Everyone filed in and sat down. The room was in total silence. No one moved. We sat for maybe ten minutes like that, as the room went gold.

The evening was hilarious, and at the very end, the last thing Rama said was a truly heartfelt thank you. He said he really, really wanted to thank us for helping him with the advertising fund for *Snowboarding to Nirvana*. He said this in a soft voice with his eyes closed, and it was totally powerful.

I sat on the beach after all this, and after awhile I went to my room and got into bed.

When I woke up I was refreshed and felt really sharp and clear. The day was beautiful. I went for a long walk along the beach, past the boundary of the resort and up the beach for a couple of miles. I was in a completely non-usual state of mind. Instead of being part of what was going on around me, I felt totally removed from the bustle, albeit a relaxed bustle, of life going on around me: couples holding hands walking along, children playing in the water along the shore, barbecues in process, friends sitting around talking, seagulls skimming the waves, dogs chasing sticks, the drone of ski-do's out on the water. All of this was going on, but was somehow enclosed in a bubble of silence. I felt as if there was some kind of distance which couldn't be measured between myself and the world around me. The overwhelming feeling I had was that everything was in an absolutely perfect balance. I was able to see that everyone was doing precisely what they were supposed to be doing, myself included, and there was a glowing light around everything. This was a really good moment that went on for hours. I felt that the light from the night before, the light from Rama, had clarified and dissolved me, and infused the world with peace and understanding.

Rama knew how to live life fully. He understood the importance of working hard to succeed and how committed, purposeful work can clarify your life. He also knew when to stop, take a break from it all, and "blow everything out of your system." I have never met anyone who could rival Rama's sense of timing, style and ability to create an unforgettable, blow-it-all-out party. He often said, of himself and of his students, "We work hard and party harder!" This was undeniably true, and whenever it seemed to Rama that his students were beginning to get heavy and were taking things a little too seriously, he would announce to us all that he was going to throw a rave party.

Now, Rama's raves were not like the typical dance marathons accompanied by excessive drug use that take place in smoky nightclubs and similar venues across the country each weekend. Nobody ever took drugs at Rama's raves, and no alcohol was served; however, everyone there became unbelievably high and transcendent. When Rama undertook any task, whether it was something he had never done before or something he had done thousands of times, he always did it in a perfect way. He was a living example of Tantric Buddhism, which teaches us to use everything in our lives as a means to attaining Enlightenment. When Rama threw a rave, he made sure that it was the biggest, loudest, most outrageous, and happiest party any of us had ever attended.

Rama's raves were always held in a totally unexpected location. We danced in some of the finest locations in all of New York City, including the Guggenheim Museum, the main branch of the New York Public Library, the Winter Garden of the World Financial Center, and the Rainbow Room in Lincoln Center, to name a few spots. Part of the fun of each party was waiting to find out what the location would be, as Rama always outdid the previous location, and we could look forward to an infusion of over-the-top surprise and delight from the inception. In each place, we were treated to an outstanding laser light show that would engulf a dance floor resounding with incredible techno music provided by one or another of New York's finest DJs, a beautiful video would be displayed on a monster-sized screen, and, always, there was impeccable catering.

At the raves, people who were usually bashful and ashamed to dance would find themselves abandoning their cares and worries and dancing for five hours straight. Even if you didn't know how to dance, it was as if the music would take over and transport you to a world of light and pure happiness. Supportively, in all this release of energy, and throughout the evening, we were served with sushi, hors d'oeuvres and truly fantastic desserts, perfect complements to the music and laser light show. Finally, exhausted and in a state of bliss, we would reluctantly depart, dragging our happy, worn-out selves back to our cars for the drive home. The joy, light, refreshment and clarity from each of these dance parties are something that I will cherish, and carry with me, always.

Rama always gave outrageous parties. One of his extravagant parties was a formal Hawaiian theme party in a five-star hotel with palm trees, hula dancers, endless exotic flowers, and eight feet tall, ominous tikis with scowling faces that lined the walls. I was enjoying the decor when Rama walked up to me and said hello. He asked if I was having a good time and if I liked his decorations. I replied that I was having an unbelievable time, but that I thought that the tikis looked a bit unhappy. He laughed and said, "I think they have a 'fuck you' attitude. I like that." Then he smiled brightly, winked at me, and gracefully strolled away.

The first rave party was the best. It was the best because no one knew what was going to happen. It was an entirely new structure and there weren't any expectations or fixed ideas. No one even knew if anyone could dance. As it turned out, over 400 people (computer professionals, no less) danced for hours and hours. I saw Rama doing things with his hands, like opening dimensional doorways, which I haven't seen at any of the other raves. The music was already playing when I got there. Some people were dancing, and some people were looking around nervously. I decided to dance a little, but I didn't really get into it. I danced for a short while, and then I decided to get something to drink. I got a cranberry juice and sat down at a table facing the dance floor. I sipped my drink and looked around at the dancers. In front of me there were some people standing. I felt myself trying to see through them for some unknown reason. Without any conscious decision, I felt that there was something I should be seeing that was right in front of me but I was missing it. I looked straight ahead and suddenly the crowds in front of me parted. It was like a veil was lifted from my eyesight and I saw Rama. He was dancing! He was moving his arms and legs and my first thought was, 'Shiva! Shiva dancing!' I know that is probably corny, but that's the only way to describe it. Shiva dancing is the Dance of Enlightenment, right? And this was Enlightenment dancing. It can't be explained. That feeling is indescribable - Enlightenment dancing.

It was our fourth and final night on the tropical island of Nevis. I had spent the last four-and-a-half days swimming, sunning, going for solitary walks on the beach, meditating, and meeting up with old friends. It was Rama's idea to host "Power Trip" excursions to different Caribbean Islands for his students and friends, and this was the second of four excursions we had in 1997. It was June, so the days were hot and dry, and the evenings were hot and humid, save for a summer breeze that would lightly creep in. But, we didn't care about the heat. We were having such a wonderful time. By day, we were going on adventures or just being alone and contemplative. By night we were eating incredible island foods offered in bountiful buffets, dancing to the Calypso beat, and then meditating and listening to Rama as he explained Buddhist philosophies in one of the conference rooms of our four-star hotel.

I'd call Nevis a magical island. I've never before experienced the feelings that I had there. On my arrival, I felt as if a ton of bricks had been lifted off of my shoulders. The lightness of the air seemed to lift me into it and hold me there. It seemed to sparkle with light. The bay, a beautiful, clear turquoise blue, caressed my body as I floated, gently holding me as a mother would a child.

I found the people of Nevis to be humble, kind and caring. There was a sense of community among them. I don't think they really want their island to become a large tourist attraction, yet they welcomed us openly. During the course of the five-day experience, I would thank the waitress or the person bringing Evian water to us as we sat in our beach chairs, and they would reply, "We are here to make you happy." They were sincere.

I think by the fourth night, having had these four-and-a-half days and three nights with friends and with Rama, we were all pretty high. We were not high in a giddy sense, but for me, being high is a subtle change in consciousness where everything is absolutely beautiful and incredibly clear. Maybe I'm seeing life as it truly is in those moments — the refinement and perfection of things as they relate to one another. Rama had planned out our evenings so that each night built upon the previous one — each night being more spectacular than the last. This fourth night, the night of the Carnival, was exceptional.

There was a red cloth walkway with small white lights leading to the large, white, open tent, which was set up on the lawn of the hotel grounds near the golf course. I felt like a princess as I walked towards the tent opening, taking in the beauty of the total effect. At the end of the walkway was the check-in table where I was given a traditional Caribbean party mask covered with green, yellow, and purple feathers, the eyeholes surrounded by dark pink sequins. As I walked into the tent, I couldn't believe my eyes or ears. The corners and periphery of the tent were decorated with large plastic palm trees with dark brown coconuts that looked real. The leaves of the trees were wide and dark green. On either side of the tent were large buffets, fit for a king (or princess), of every kind of food imaginable - fish, pork, beef, vegetables, rice.... The Calypso band was magnificently playing "One Love" by Bob Marley - how apropos! The greens of the palm leaves on the band members' multicolored tropical-island shirts exactly matched the green on the decorative palm trees. It was all just so exquisitely and perfectly arranged like a fine puzzle that was complete. I sat at one of the round tables set in the middle section of the tent. (The front area, which was for dancing, was being well used). I turned around to take a full-spectrum look at everything once again and saw a friend dancing at her table. I thought to myself, 'Wow! She looks like a goddess!' I turned a little further and saw Rama happily strolling along the back of the tent. I beamed at him. I think he must have felt my thoughts because he beamed back and nodded just slightly, as if to confirm my feelings at that moment.

I danced and ate and drank and danced some more. There were little tambourines being passed around, so I played one for a little while. Then, it came time for the limbo. The line was a really long; I had my turn to make it under the stick only once. Not long after the contest began, a group of island dancers joined us on the dance floor. Dressed in traditional clothing, they wore tall, round pill-box-type hats, long tunics and pants, all of brightly colored strips of deep red, yellow, and green. The dancers were of all ages - from people in their 60's to children who looked to be about six years old. It really struck me that they would be so kind as to entertain us with their traditional dance. The look on the faces of the children was of pure gentleness. I just watched and clapped in support of their sharing maybe the deepest parts of their heritage with us. I felt a reverence towards them and their culture. Although a part of me eventually wanted to join in with the continued festivities of the limbo and traditional dance as some of my friends were, I couldn't. Something was drawing me deeper and deeper into myself and into the respectful compassion or reverence that exists there (something that in my hurried and somewhat self-centered lifestyle I don't often feel). I struggled again for a moment to try to join in to the party atmosphere. Then, I looked over to my right and there was Rama, maybe ten feet away, quietly clapping and talking to a student while watching the activities. I then knew that it was his presence that brought me into that deep place and held me there.

I will always be grateful for that experience. It is something I can treasure and go back to. I will never forget the image of his gentle being, his always-present being, ever guiding us to a deeper, more true self.

Parties with Rama were experiences that I'll never forget. The reason is that I sensed changes in myself at many different levels. I had the most incredible experience during one of our trips to the Caribbean - the Nevis trip. It was our last night. An awesome band was playing very lively music. Everyone, including Rama, was dancing. It was hot, the place was beautiful, and the food was amazing. As I began to dance, I immediately felt I had entered a different realm. The difference was so noticeable that I went back to where I was before in order to reenter the dance floor and re-experience the sensation. I began to dance again and noticed that not just my body was dancing. My soul was dancing, filled to the brim with the most pure bliss. I had been transported to a place where I had no awareness of myself. Everything seemed so simple and weightless. Life itself was so simple. I felt I was "seeing" the reality of life without the usual weight of my mind and personality, desires and aversions. It was a timeless moment where I felt completely impersonal and detached. I was aware of everyone and Rama. We were all very much together in this realm, united by our bliss. All I could do was jump. I jumped higher and higher to release the surge of happiness that had overwhelmed me, the urge to celebrate and thank Rama for that moment. I looked around and there were many other people jumping too. I felt united, as in a family, where we all understood each other, and acknowledged the wonderfulness of our teacher and our fortune to experience those precious moments with him.

In early 1996, Rama took a small group of people to a Caribbean island on a scuba diving trip. We spent our days under water experiencing the breathtaking beauty of bright corals and colorful fish or exploring the island's volcano. We discovered that the island had a special magic, power and purity that has since been difficult to find anywhere else. Our evenings were spent with Rama discussing Buddhism, meditation, and business on a terrace that has a spectacular view of the surrounding islands and is lit at night by the moon and stars alone. Those evenings with Rama are indescribable. By the end of the trip I felt a peace and happiness that I had never before experienced.

On our last night on the terrace with Rama, he asked us to tell him about our day. When it was my turn, I told him that I had been scuba diving. I described a moment underwater when I became completely overwhelmed by the beauty and perfection of life. I was part of everything and everything was part of me. There were no thoughts in my mind. I experienced perfect happiness, bliss and peace. As I told Rama my story, I was brought back to that moment of perfect meditation and once again experienced complete ecstasy. Rama paused for a moment and then, nodding his head, he responded, "I know exactly what you mean. I live in that state of perfection and happiness all of the time." Rama gave me a small glimpse into the mind of Enlightenment and I will forever be grateful to him.

First Meetings

The meditation was over. I didn't want it to end, the feeling of no-body, no-mind. My spirit had touched another place, somewhere empty and quiet, a place of safety. After I bowed my thanks, I felt waves stream through my body. While feeling them, I pictured waves of light capping, eddying out, and then returning once more. When they ended, I opened my eyes and looked up at the circular stained glass window that dominated the sanctuary of the church. The red portions of the stained-glass window grabbed my attention. The dazzle reminded me that there were physical objects, people, and a world outside of what was happening to me.

I closed my eyes again. All I could see was white light. I was empty other than this light. This was who I really was. I knew that. The meditation teacher sitting lotus-style in front of me had brought me up, out of my normal state of consciousness, then back to myself. I wanted to feel this way forever.

He turned off the music, the Tangerine Dream tape, and we sat in silence. It seemed like he didn't want the moment to end either. If I was in ecstasy, how must he, the conduit of the meditation, feel? I couldn't imagine how he could function as he clicked open his briefcase and carefully put the tape back into its case. That done, he closed his eyes again and smiled. He was somewhere else, his body was in front of me, but he was gone. Then he opened his eyes, completely present and aware. He joked, told us we were higher than we might imagine, and cautioned us to splash some water on our face before heading home. He reminded us to meditate throughout the week, then walked off the stage.

I took a deep breath and thought how lucky I was to have met Rama, and smiled how it had happened so unexpectedly.

One night, over a year before, I had dreamt of mountains, tall, majestic mountains, snow-covered mountains. Only this wasn't a normal dream, it was tangible, vivid—like everyday reality. In this clear, awake-dream, I was on a pilgrimage. I was intently searching for someone or someplace, and the intensity of the search took away all my fears. I climbed mountain trails, not letting the snow bother me. I wasn't cold; I was so focused in my search, I hardly realized it was snowing. Then I came to the place, the structure I had been looking for. It was a temple, a Zen temple. I puzzled at this, thinking that Japanese temples weren't found in the Himalayas, where I knew I was. My questioning mind stopped as a calm and blissful feeling, which emanated from the temple, flooded me. Then, as the dream began fading, I remembered a technique I had read about recently, and asked the dream where I could find the temple. Not an answer but an intuitive knowing came to my mind, as clearly as if I had read the answer in a book. 'San Francisco,' I sleepily thought to myself, 'I can find all this in San Francisco.'

It in the morning, the dream's clarity amazed and delighted me, but it didn't make sense. San Francisco? Finding that bliss and staying with it longer was something I wanted to do—I had to find the temple—but I would have preferred a command to trek to the Himalayas or even to British Columbia. Living most of my life in Northern California, I knew San Francisco too well to think it held mysteries. San Francisco?

Months later, my friend brought home a poster of Rama and threw it on the kitchen table. I was sitting at the table, after breakfast, intent on finishing the San Francisco Chronicle. But she aimed well, so that the newsletter landed between the Chronicle and me, and I was forced to look up.

"See what I picked up from the Co-op." She meant the Berkeley Co-op, a radical sounding name to an otherwise staid market, not too different from Lucky's or Safeway. "It seems like it might be interesting. Do you want to go?"

I looked at the poster. A young, curly-haired man stared back at me. His name was Atmananda and he was giving a series of meditation lectures in San Francisco, at the George Moscone Convention Center. We had already missed the first class, but there were two more sessions left. "Journey through the Void" read the caption above the cherubic face. Then underneath the picture was his resume. Zen Teacher in Kyoto, 17th century. High Priest in Egypt. High Priest in Atlantis. This was outrageous. There was no metaphysical poster in all of Berkeley that could come close to this.

"Sure, let's go." I didn't know why I was saying this. There seemed no logical reason to want to go. The poster was, after all, absurd. But she, the cynic, had suggested going and I agreed. We looked at each other in surprise.

We didn't change our minds about going to the "Journey through the Void" lecture. After reading the newsletter that Rama's organization, named Lakshmi, produced, I wanted to go even more. The front-page article was "Why Don't More Women Attain Enlightenment?" In all the women's groups I had belonged to for the past ten years, I had never heard that question asked; Enlightenment was outside our topics of discussion. I guessed that not too many spiritual groups had thought about the topic either.

Despite my resolve, it seemed strange driving, in the drizzling rain, to the Moscone Center for the lecture. I felt disconnected from what I had come to call myself—that logical part that is in control, organizes and plans her life, and knows what she is doing. This lecture didn't fit into the plan and yet I was almost there.

Outside the convention room, four or five well-dressed, smiling people sat at a table and greeted me. One took my $4 in exchange for an entrance ticket. They looked like college students, though maybe a bit older. I guess I felt reassured: they weren't wearing saris and didn't seem spaced out.

Inside, the chairs were lined up in rows, lecture style. My friend and I took seats at the back of the room in case we wanted to leave early. Music I had never heard before, electronic music (I was later told) by a group named Tangerine Dream was playing. Some people were talking to each other, others had their eyes closed. I guessed they were meditating. The curly-haired Rama had not arrived yet.

Then Rama made his entrance. He seemed so familiar to me...it gnawed at me where I might have seen him before. He was dressed L.A.-preppy, which made sense since he lived in L.A.—Malibu to be exact. He wore shorts and a white v-neck sweater with a stripe bordering the 'v', like the kind tennis players wear at the country club. It wasn't my style.

Before talking, he sat with both legs folded into each other on a table at the front of the conference room. The table was covered by a multicolored afghan, something a Midwestern grandmother might knit. Later he told us his sitting style was called a full-lotus, but assured us we didn't need to sit like that if we wanted to meditate.

He began with a lecture. The main point was that yes, the world is a mess, crazy, upside-down. We are ruining the planet's ecosystem. We are breeding more than the real estate can handle. There is racial hatred. Half of the world's citizens, women, are socialized to feel that they are second-class. Most people care more about money than they do about the Spirit.

In spite of all this, there is a practice accessible to anyone. It will help you deal with the craziness of the world. The practice, which is meditation, will enable you to see the beauty around you and in yourself. It will help you to be kinder, to have more patience, to be balanced. Meditation must be done in a grounded way, though. For example, it is important to have a solid career, this will help ground your meditation practice. He said that many of us have been drawn to meditation because we practiced it in other lives.

He gave examples from recent movies and from modern life—driving on a freeway, going to public high school, shopping at the grocery store. He was funny. He was poignant. I instinctively knew he was telling the truth.

Then we meditated. He told us to close our eyes and listen to the music. He explained that in a public setting like this, there were many different vibrations. The music helped to neutralize the swirl and gave us a central point on which to concentrate. We were to listen to the music, no more. If we became distracted, we were to put our attention back on the music. The song would last for approximately five minutes.

He took a big breath and closed his eyes. I did the same. I tried to listen to "Chariots of Fire", the song that was playing, but it was impossible. One millisecond I listened and the next minute my mind was hijacked by thoughts. They ranged from: 'What am I doing here? I can't do this. Why am I even trying?' to: 'What will we do when this is over? Should we go out?'

Finally the meditation was over. Rama told us to open our eyes slowly. Then he began speaking. Surprisingly, I noticed I was calmer. My mind wasn't in such whirl. He said that he meditated so well that even if we could barely sit still, we felt the effect of his meditation. This didn't seem like bragging to me, it was the truth.

There was another meditation, again about five minutes long. This time we looked at him during the song instead of closing our eyes. Again, my mind chattered, though maybe not so much. At the end of the meditation he asked us what our experience had been. Several people said they felt calmer and liked watching their thoughts slow. Other people stated matter-of-factly that they had seen purple and gold light coming from Rama and flowing out into the audience. One woman said Rama had turned into an American Indian warrior during the meditation, with a headdress of feathers and paint on his face. To yet another he had become a Hindu god whose name I can't remember.

Rama made short comments after each person spoke, such as, "Oh, you saw that?" or, "Yeah, isn't the gold light neat?" Then he described how we could begin a meditation practice at home.

Rama ended the evening by saying he had come to San Francisco despite the death threats he had received prior to the meditation. He came, he said, because there were people here who had been his students in past lives and were drawing him. He said he had been coming to us in our dreams to help prepare us for studying with him again in this life. I remembered the Himalayan dream, then dropped the thought to keep listening. Rama said he was starting a Center in San Francisco in addition to the existing Centers in San Diego and Los Angeles. Anyone who wanted to apply could meet with him now, at the front of the room. But this wouldn't be the final opportunity: there would be a lecture next week, as well as an intensive meditation. 'Good,' my cautious side thought, 'I'll wait to see how I feel next week.'

We walked out into the night. It was still drizzling. I knew I had met my teacher, though he wasn't at all what I was expecting.

"You know," I told my friend, "I feel like I'm home." Smiling, she nodded her head in agreement.

Walking to class, I noticed a poster advertising three classes in meditation and self-discovery, taught by Dr. Frederick Lenz. The topics were beginning and intermediate mediation. I had never practiced meditation before, nor did I know what it was, but something felt right about the 8 1/2" x 11" yellow poster. So I noted the time, date and location, and attended the three classes.

I arrived a little early for the initial class and found a seat by the aisle half way back on the right side of the room. It was a standard university classroom. There were windows along the right wall, metal file cabinets in the back, two isles of desks, all facing toward the front where there was a black board on the wall, and a large table and chair for the instructor. A few other college students walked in and sat down. After a while, a tall curly-haired man with long strides entered through the door at the back of the room and walked up the aisle toward the front desk. Another gentleman followed him, carrying a tape player. Dr. Lenz walked around the desk to face us, smiled, said hello and remarked on what a beautiful day it was. The tape player was placed on the desk and plugged in.

Dr. Lenz told us that meditation was a lot of fun, and that at a certain point in a person's life they seem to find themselves drawn to the practice of meditation and self-discovery. He said that if a person is interested in meditation, they have probably done this before in other lives. The things he said felt familiar to me, comfortable. Dr. Lenz described meditation as a practice of stilling the mind, eventually stopping all thought. He described the world as a place where everyone is psychic and projects psychic energy. Everyone is feeling and experiencing the thoughts, feelings and emotions of everyone else. He said that this can get to be confusing, especially for someone who meditates, because they are trying to become more psychic, more sensitive, more aware.

He told us not to just take his word for it, but to discover for ourselves if what he said was true or not. He described a way: to take a walk in the woods, someplace where there were few if any people, and to observe our minds, observe the thoughts and feelings we had. Then, he suggested we take a walk in a crowded area, like a shopping mall, and observe our thoughts. He recommended that we do a comparison, and chances were that we would see that we were experiencing the thoughts, feelings and emotions of everyone around us.

He said that meditation helps a person to determine what it is they think and feel, separate from what other people around them are thinking and feeling. Because everyone is psychic and because the world is becoming more and more crowded, there are fewer and fewer places where a person can go to clear out, to be alone for awhile. "Meditation helps to create this space," Dr. Lenz explained.

Dr. Lenz described our bodies as being made up of a physical body, arms, legs, torso, head, as well as what he called a subtle physical body. He said that the subtle physical body is a body of light which extends about six inches from our physical body, and which surrounds our physical body. Some people call this a person's aura.

"You can see this body of light," he said. "Auras have different colors. The subtle physical body also has a vibration. A healthy aura vibrates very quickly. You may not have consciously noticed this before," he said, "but if you think through your experiences of meeting people, we tend to be drawn to people who have clean, healthy auras, ones that vibrate more quickly."

Dr. Lenz began to explain the meditation practices we were going to learn. He said that we would be focusing on chakras, energy centers in the subtle physical body that are associated to positions on the physical body. He said that there are seven primary chakras, or energy centers, on the body, and that these are areas where the energy lines of the subtle body meet. There are many energy centers all over the body. This is known to the practitioners of acupuncture and acupressure. The first of the seven primary chakras is located at the base of the spine. The second is located in the area of the spleen. The third chakra is called the navel chakra and is located about one inch below the navel. This is the area of will power and is used in the practice of martial arts to draw on the power of will. The fourth chakra is called the heart chakra, or Anahata. It is located right in the center of the chest and is the area of love, beauty and balance. It is the fourth of the seven primary chakras and is located approximately at the midway point between them.

He said that the way to locate the heart chakra was by holding one index finger up in the air, and then simultaneously saying the word 'me' while gently touching the index finger to the center of the chest. Dr. Lenz had a large beaming smile as he said, "Me," and pointed his index finger to the center of his chest. We all tried this a few times. He told us that the fifth chakra is located at the base of the throat and is associated with the creative arts. He mentioned that this chakra was accessed by many of the artists in the days of the Renaissance. The sixth chakra is called the third eye or Agni chakra, and is located on the forehead, between eyes and about one inch above the bridge of the nose. This energy center is the area of knowledge, intuition and wisdom. Dr. Lenz said that the seventh of the primary chakras was not associated with a part of the physical body, but was above the crown of the head. It is called the crown chakra and is accessed by Enlightened Beings.

The meditation techniques he taught focused on three of the chakras: the navel chakra, the heart chakra, and the third eye or Agni chakra. He reviewed each one, and had us feel those three places on our body. Dr. Lenz explained that by focusing on these areas, we would be accessing the energies associated with them, strengthening those energies and making them more available to us to use in our daily lives.

Dr. Lenz then described the first meditation technique we were going to learn. He said that meditation is a practice of stilling the mind. When the mind becomes still and quiet, the world goes away and we get in touch with a very deep part of ourselves. It is a quiet, still, beautiful place filled with light. When we still our minds in meditation, we enter this place and it energizes us, renews us, gives us experiences of hope, light and magic. "For the first technique," he said, "I want you to imagine a red rose in the center of your chest, a big red rose that is closed at first. Then imagine that the first layer of petals open and fill the inside of your chest. Then see the second layer of petals open and expand inside your chest. After that, see the third, and continue until the entire rose has opened and fills the inside of your chest in the area of the heart chakra."

"While we do this, I will play some music," Dr. Lenz said. He said that he uses the music for a few reasons. One, so that people who are not used to sitting and meditating will not be self-conscious about disturbing others when they need to shift positions or cough. He uses music that people do not normally associate with specific experiences or emotions in their life, which might cause them to think about those times and experiences. "So close your eyes," he said, "sit up straight. It is important that you sit up straight. If you need to, you can rest your back against the back of the chair, but it is important to sit up straight. Just fold your hands comfortably in your lap and have your feet flat on the floor. You just want to relax and sit up straight. If you get tired, just sit back and listen to the music. If thoughts come in and out of your mind, just ignore them, go back and focus on the rose in the center of your chest."

"Okay, close your eyes," he said, as he turned on the music. "We will just meditate for an hour or two - just kidding," he joked. "We will meditate for just a few minutes." Then he was silent and I turned my focus to the rose in the center of my chest.

I saw the petals open and felt the inside of my chest expand. The energy from the rose and from the area of my heart chakra expanded beyond the boundaries of my chest. Thoughts came in and out of my mind, and I lost and regained focus of the rose, but I never lost the amazing feeling that was inside me. Dr. Lenz turned off the music and told us to open our eyes, sit back and relax. The time had passed so quickly. I opened my eyes and looked up at

Dr. Lenz at the front of the room. I don't know if he was actually looking at me, but I looked at him and saw this huge grin on his face and noticed that I too had a huge grin on my face. My mind was quiet and clear, and I felt quietly happy. This was something new. I do not remember ever feeling this way before, yet it felt so comfortable and natural.

Dr. Lenz spoke some more about meditation and how the world had become a crowded place, difficult for finding quiet places to meditate. "Long ago," he said, "people serious about meditation and self-discovery went to the Himalayas to meditate in the quiet and solitude of the caves in the mountains. We do not have as many of these kinds of places here, and the world is becoming more and more overcrowded. So we are learning to find the quiet places in our own minds, and at the same time strengthening the mind through focus and concentration."

The second meditation technique Dr. Lenz described was to begin by seeing a blue ball of light entering through the third eye. He told us to take the blue ball of light and bring it down from the third eye to the heart chakra. Then repeat this a few times, seeing a blue ball of light entering the third eye, and bringing the blue ball of light from the third eye to the heart chakra. After a while, he told us to just rest our attention at the place of the third eye. We lightly touched the area of the heart chakra and of the third eye. Dr. Lenz reminded us to sit up straight, to close our eyes, and if we began to think thoughts, to just ignore them and return to focusing on the blue ball of light. He started the music and I began to meditate.

When Dr. Lenz turned off the music, told us to open our eyes, sit back and relax, I felt very clear and energized. We did a third short meditation, then Dr. Lenz reminded us of the next meeting place and time. At the end of class, I walked by Dr. Lenz in order to exit through the front door. He was smiling as I passed, and I could feel this ridiculously large smile on my face.

One day in 1981, during my junior year at UCLA, I read an advertisement in the student newspaper publicizing an upcoming meditation workshop series, which would be conducted on campus by a spiritual teacher. The ad featured a resume chronicling the teacher's past life experience as the head of monastic orders in India, Japan and Tibet. The ad also described the interaction between the teacher and workshop participants. The teacher would enter into a high state of meditation known as samadhi and from that state he would channel peace and light to all present. I read those extraordinary claims without the slightest trace of skepticism. Meditating with a highly evolved Master didn't seem extraordinary at all; it just seemed like the natural thing to do. Immediately, I decided to attend.

The first workshop took place on a weekday afternoon in a lecture hall in one of the science buildings on the southern part of campus. About fifteen people were seated when I arrived. Perhaps fifteen more trickled in before the workshop started. Most were college kids like myself. A few were older New Age movement types. Rama arrived about fifteen minutes after the appointed hour. He made his entrance from the rear, strolling down the stairs with a happy smile and an easy gait. He was a tall man in his early thirties, with a long mane of curly brown hair, dressed in California casual mode. He carried a "boom box" portable cassette player and a can of Sunkist orange soda. He put his things down on the counter and seated himself there in a cross-legged position, facing us.

He began the workshop with some light remarks and logistics. Then he lectured a bit on kundalini energy, the seven primary chakras, and the states of samadhi and Nirvana. Next, he instructed us to meditate with our eyes open, focused gently on him. The meditation lasted for about ten or fifteen minutes, and was followed by a discussion session. This cycle of lecture, meditation and discussion was repeated twice, so that there were three meditation sessions in the workshop.

I had read about the concepts Rama lectured on before in one place or another, but I had never experienced anything like the meditation sessions with him. During each session we meditated to electronic music by a band called Tangerine Dream, which Rama played on his "boom box". And during each session, the room filled with sparkling golden light as soon as Rama began to meditate. But each meditation was unique.

The first session was like a ride at Disneyland. The room tilted from side to side like a seesaw, as Rama slid from one end to the other. He also seemed to get smaller and larger, and in addition to the golden light, my entire visual field was incandescent.

104

The second meditation was still and pristine. Rama transformed before my eyes from a modern young Californian Caucasian man to a traditional, older Japanese man dressed in black.

The third meditation was the most intense. During this meditation, Rama focused his gaze, for a moment, on each of member of the audience individually. When he looked at me, I felt as though I had been struck by a bolt of energy.

Rama closed the session by thanking us and informing us of the dates of the next workshops in the series. I don't remember how I felt as I left the auditorium, but I think it's safe to say that my attitude was astonishingly blase. I had no idea that this encounter had been the most important of my entire life.

Later that evening, I sat alone in my room to meditate. I closed my eyes and suddenly it seemed that time had stopped and that I was at the edge of the universe, or the edge of my mind, looking out over the abyss. The feeling was magnificent. It was also quite frightening.

Over the next year and a half or so, I casually attended Rama's workshops whenever they were held at UCLA. Rama had founded a spiritual school called Lakshmi, named in honor of the Indian goddess. On several occasions, in a very nonchalant manner, Rama made applications to study with him on a more formal and personal basis (under the auspices of the Lakshmi organization) available to workshop participants. At the time, I wasn't interested. Once he invited workshop participants to a larger meeting with his students in San Diego. I declined, thinking that it would be too much of a hassle to get to San Diego, as I had no car. This is ironic in retrospect. In the years that followed, I have packed up and moved across the United States three times to study with Rama; I have flown from coast to coast dozens of times to attend a two or four night seminar with him; and I have traveled to Europe to lecture on meditation and beginning Buddhist practice.

About a year and a half after first meeting Rama, my interest in studying with him began to intensify. He had begun to produce beautiful, high quality, full color brochure kits that were distributed to attendees of his public workshops. Cassette tape recordings of his talks on dozens of spiritual and occult topics were available, and he had also written two books of spiritual insights. I listened to the cassettes and read the brochures and books over and over again. They were so inspiring. I had also begun to meditate each day.

I decided to apply to study with Rama. The Lakshmi student application included short answer questions and essay questions. I remember filling out the application without really knowing why I was doing it, but I sent it in anyway, and a few weeks later I received a letter from Rama, which thanked me for the application, but rejected me. Somehow I was not disappointed. I continued to meditate on my own and I saw Rama at public workshops whenever I could.

Rama produced new brochure sets and tapes often, and each was more sophisticated and professional than the last. Sometimes there would be a special enclosure with the brochure set, like a flyer with quotes by Rama. At one workshop a book was distributed. The book was called *The Last Incarnation*, and it was composed of accounts of Rama's students' experiences with him, which were written by the students themselves. This book made an incredible impact on me. I related to what I read in ways that I don't think I really understand. I just began to believe that I was destined to be Rama's student.

I applied to study with Rama again, and he sent me the same rejection letter. This time I was actually surprised, but I was not bitter. In the letter, Rama said something like "as you probably know, I have been meditating intensely on your soul over the past few days." In fact, after mailing both of my applications, the golden light I saw around Rama at his workshops filled my room during my daily meditations. These were very high times for me. Inwardly, I understood that if he declined my application it was for the best. Or perhaps I simply felt so good from all the public meditations, books and cassette tapes that were available that the rejection didn't matter.

Several of the accounts in *The Last Incarnation* made references to Malibu. These accounts indicated that Rama perceived that Malibu was a very powerful place, that he had chosen to live there, and that he had recommended the area to many of his students. Often I had visited Santa Monica beach, and had gazed at the majesty of the Santa Monica mountain range as it jutted out to the sea a few miles north. Malibu was on the other side of those mountains, and although I had lived in Los Angeles for several years, I had been there only once, at night. Now I was drawn there. Somewhere in the back of my mind I thought that I might meet Rama there.

So, one afternoon I drove up. My destination was Charmlee Park, a public land reserve in the hills. I had read in *The Last Incarnation* that Rama had once invited a few of his students there for a special field trip. It seemed like a good place to visit.

While rounding one of the curves in the road, I caught a glimpse of a red Porsche parked on the plateau above. I had read in *The Last Incarnation* that Rama owned a red Porsche with a little plastic frog mounted on the dashboard. Could this be Rama's car? My heart began to beat a little faster. I felt like the archetypal spiritual seeker who treks on foot high into the Himalayas to find an old guru in a cave. But my story had a late twentieth century, Southern California twist.

When I reached the plateau I parked my scooter, then walked over to the Porsche. The frog was there on the dash. This was Rama's car! My heart began pounding in my chest. I noticed footprints leading from Rama's car to a path, which led into the forest. I followed the footprints to a tree outside the forested area and sat down to wait for Rama. I tried to meditate, but I was far too excited. My mind was exploding with thoughts of what I should say to him, and what he might say to me.

Perhaps ten minutes went by in this way. Then I heard footsteps. Rama walked out of the forest. He was wearing shorts and sneakers and had taken off his shirt. I stood up and walked toward him waving. After attending dozens of his workshops, listening for hours to his talks on tape, reading three of his books, and applying twice to be his student, I felt that I knew him. But to him I was just another face in the crowd. I felt a bit awkward. He looked at me warily. His eyes were diffuse, as though he was a million miles away. A brief dialogue ensued. I was oblivious to it at the time, but looking back I can see that Rama was in such a high state of attention that it was difficult for him to speak to me.

First I introduced myself, and he reciprocated. Then I babbled rather incoherently about *The Last Incarnation* and the Porsche, and he looked at me as though he didn't quite understand. At last I told him that I had attended his workshop the night before. He smiled and asked, "Did you enjoy it?" I answered that it was "appropriate." He made polite conversation with me for awhile. Suddenly I thought of an incident that had occurred the night before. He repeated something, which I had heard him say on several previous occasions — that people who tend to act as though they are spiritual, actually are not spiritual at all. For the first time, I realized that I fit into that category. I told him about my discovery. He said, "Yeah, a lot of my students are that way." Then I told him that I had applied to be his student before. He gazed at me intently for a moment, as though he was surveying my past lives or recalling my previous applications, and then he sort of smiled as though he saw something that he recognized. Finally, he said softly as though to himself, "It wasn't the right time." He smiled mischievously and said, "This is an auspicious meeting, don't you think?" At the time the words didn't really register in me, but I sensed what he meant, and I said, "Yes." He told me not to be discouraged because I had been turned down before. After a bit more polite conversation he bid me good day and got into his car. He waved a long arm through the sunroof, and I waved back. Then he drove away.

At the seminar that evening, Rama told those of us in attendance who were not his students that he felt we were well-suited for the study of Enlightenment. To emphasize that his statement was no mere platitude, he defied any of us to recall him saying something similar in the past. I could not recall hearing anything to that effect before, and no one else seemed to either. On the way out that evening I picked up a Lakshmi student application. I filled it out carefully and mailed it. A few weeks later, I received a letter indicating that my application had been accepted.

The magazine I picked up at the local health food store where I worked was called "Self Discovery" and had a picture of a girl sitting in meditation on the hood of a Porsche parked at the beach. I was intrigued. On the back page was an almost full-page picture of a preppy-looking guy named Rama in his late twenties, wearing a turtleneck sweater and smiling broadly at the camera. He had a halo-like tangle of curly blonde hair and piercing blue-gray eyes. He was apparently the main attraction of this Self Discovery program.

I was on my lunch break, relaxing in the back of the California beach-town health food store where I spent my work hours cutting and weighing cheese, unpacking organic fruits and vegetables, restocking the unfinished wooden shelves, and cleaning up after the bizarre clientele. The man in the picture seemed to be looking right at me, reminding me of the alluring eyes of a famous fashion model I admired.

As I gazed at the young man's engaging eyes, I suddenly lost feeling in my arms and legs. They went numb. I heard a faint buzzing in my ears and the photograph seemed to come to life, as if I were looking at a live television screen, not a magazine. His whole face came to life, and I was afraid I had eaten something terrible that was making me hallucinate.

I looked anxiously at my hands, and they were calmly holding the magazine, though I couldn't feel them. My mind seemed unable to formulate thoughts, and I felt my awareness telescoping down to the smiling face. It filled my entire field of vision. I felt a pressure in my chest, it was a little painful, and I breathed shallowly. As my anxiety level over my sudden attack increased, I looked back at the picture: I could swear that the young man in the photograph was laughing at me.

Two weeks later, on October 10, 1982, I decided to try and meet Rama. I had tried gazing at the photograph a few times since my initial experience, but it was not lending any further out-of-body experiences.

I had prepared myself by reading through the entire Self Discovery magazine. Rama claimed to be a "multi-incarnation" teacher with a resume that included stints in many of the high holy places known for eastern religion, magic and mysticism. Tibetan Buddhist Dalai Lama, Japanese Zen Master, and even High Priest of the Atlantean and Egyptian Mystery Schools were listed among his accomplishments. I assumed that he was probably telling the truth, based on the way his picture had sparked to life in front of my eyes.

I underestimated the commute from my beach-town one-bedroom house to San Francisco's Grace Cathedral, and arrived at the seminar about thirty minutes late. Two extremely polite, but unyielding bouncer-types informed me that the chapel was completely full, not even standing room available. My heart sank. I turned to leave, but was still resolved to get into the meeting; after all, I had driven two hours and needed to find out if my experience with the picture had been a fantasy, a hallucination, or an actual out-of-body experience.

So I strolled around the outer corridors of the cathedral, pretending interest in the window displays of history and important benefactors. Every few minutes I heard an outburst of laughter from inside the chapel. The two bouncers noticed me lurking around, but they ignored me.

After what seemed like hours, the doors to the chapel finally opened and young people with bright smiles, many of them laughing, came streaming into the outer hallway where soft drinks, cookies, and fruit awaited them. It was a nice spread of food, I thought, especially considering that the meeting was free. They were talking excitedly in small groups, probably about something interesting Rama had said. I discreetly moved toward the open chapel doors, hoping to sneak in during the break.

As I stared intently at my objective, Rama suddenly appeared at the door. The first thing I noticed was how tall he was — at least six-foot-three, and maybe taller. He wore a red silk jacket with what looked like dragons on it, and his tanned face was dominated by a long aquiline nose, a strong square chin, and wide- set eyes that now appeared to be half closed. The sight of him made me catch my breath for a moment — he emanated strength and elegance. His emergence electrified the room; like a famous movie star walking into a high-school reunion of lawyers, shipbuilders, housewives and architects. I decided to abandon my immediate plan, because maybe I could just ask him directly what had happened to me.

Magically, Rama started sauntering in my direction, and in a moment was actually standing within a few feet of me. Another person stepped between us and started asking him for advice on a personal matter. I heard him say a few words to the effect that he didn't provide personal advice, but would always recommend that a person learn how to meditate and practice selfless giving whenever possible. I kept my eyes downcast and tried not to eavesdrop.

A moment later though, he was standing in front of me looking at me quizzically, like a scientist looking at an experiment that has gone awry. "Hi there!" he said, as if we were old friends. I responded enthusiastically, "Hi!" I was about to ask my question when I looked at his eyes, and I began to have the out-of-body experience again: my body went numb, my thoughts stopped, and I lost sight of everything except him. I seemed to be surrounded by a powerful field of light that was emanating from him and passing into me. It was the most wonderful thing I had ever experienced. The whole room disappeared and I was experiencing only a golden stream of light passing from him to me and surrounding me in an incredible aura of purity and great joy. It was a type of ecstasy that I had always longed for. I didn't want it to ever stop. But it did.

He was still looking at me with a bemused expression. I was unable to speak, so I just let my eyes fall, and looked at his chest, which was broad and covered with the shiny red Chinese fabric from his silk jacket. He said, "Meditation starts in the heart." Then he tapped my chest a few times with his forefinger. It was a very gentle gesture, but I it seemed to penetrate my heart and touch my soul. Again, I had nothing to say, and felt dumb because I consider myself a very verbal person. Finally I managed to say, "Thank you." He smiled and moved on to talk with another group of people.

I decided to go home. I felt a little weak. Before I could leave, though, one of the other attendees approached me. "Wow," he said, "Rama was talking to you for a long time. What did he say?" I told him that Rama had only said that meditation starts in the heart. The fellow then told me that Rama was accepting students, and he (the attendee) was planning to submit an application. "Are you going to become his student?" he asked me. "I feel like I already am his student," I replied.

I hold dear the memory of my experience the first time I saw Rama. It was at SUNY Purchase in a large auditorium. I was sitting towards the back with several other people and wondering, "Who is that blonde guy with round, mirrored sun glasses, sitting in a chair in the middle of the stage?" With a name like Rama, I was definitely expecting someone entirely different!

I remember feeling very giddy initially. Apparently, Rama was in one of his super extra funny moods that evening. I remember laughing the entire evening at all of his jokes and sarcasm. He had a superior talent for mixing deep spiritual teachings with outrageous humor. I remember listening to his every word, looking at him and being completely at peace. I felt filled up inside. For the first time in my life I felt like I was truly home. I felt a joy and delight, which I never knew was possible. I remember the bright clarity of the light around him. I felt this light in my heart and was overwhelmingly happy. At the time I knew nothing about Enlightenment or Eastern yogic practices. I simply knew with all the innocence of my mind and the feeling in my heart, that Rama embodied something that was beautiful, infinitely spacious and loving, and absolutely beyond comprehension.

This love of Rama's came in so many different forms. Sometimes it was simply a reminder to floss your teeth, cut out fat from your diet and exercise every day! Other times it was hours long talks on dharma, the truth. Always, his love was and is the most perfect reminder that we are already Enlightened, we are already perfect. Above all things, tirelessly and at great pain and cost to his physical self, he nurtured us with every fiber of his being to help everyone remember the truth of their own perfect divinity.

My spirit has been uplifted. My heart aches with gratitude. As a result of my experiences with Rama and his teachings, my life has become the fulfillment of a dream that magic is real and God's love is infinite, timeless and expressed in all things.

I attended my first meditation class, given by one of Rama's San Francisco students, on a Thursday night, then found myself on a plane to Los Angeles the following Tuesday. I had borrowed a suitcase, packed the new formal dress I'd bought with my rent money, then we were off to the elegant Four Seasons Hotel. This was just a surprise adventure. I had no idea my life was about to change forever!

On a beautiful outdoor garden terrace, the group of about 300 formally dressed and very animated people mingled before dinner. Hardly bothering to hide my skepticism, I quietly moved among them, checking out these people who had obviously been taken in by the latest New Age craze.

That was when Rama walked by me for the first time. Suddenly, everything shifted, and the very air seemed freer. For just a moment my mind's eye beheld a city with buildings like none I'd ever seen before. The whole atmosphere infused with a sparkly feeling of magic. And then it was gone, like an ocean breeze that blows in on your face, bringing a hint of sea smells, refreshing you. Then Rama came into view, but I didn't realize who he was - no one had told me what he looked like. I thought to myself, "That guy must be a very powerful business man."

Then dinner began. A sumptuous buffet feast awaited us, in an elegant banquet hall filled with large, round tables. The tall, handsome, beautifully dressed "businessman" walked to the front of the room, sat down and began to speak. "That's him?" I thought, a bit perplexed. His talk delighted me - he was down to earth and hilariously funny, and what he said seemed uncommonly wise. Not at all what I'd imagined.

When he invited the audience to ask questions, I had come prepared with one, a test. "Why do you teach?" The "right" answer (in my mind) was something like, "Because God tells me to," or, "Because it is the Dharma." Rama said, "Because there's nothing good on television." Everyone laughed.

Part two of the plan to see if Rama really might be Enlightened was to stand next to him for a while. I didn't intend to talk to him, just observe him more closely, to see if he really could be so different from everyone else. When Rama took a break from speaking, some people gathered around to ask more personal questions. I surreptitiously edged into the group.

He talked to each person, then turned to me. "Hi!" he said. His whole body said "Hi!" Waves of powerful, ecstatic energy surged into me from his body; I'd never experienced anything like it. I backed away a step, my mind a blank. "Uh...um...I-I-I don't have any questions right now!" I stammered. "That's good!" he said, then turned to the next person. My question was definitely answered!

My first meeting with Rama was at a formal dinner seminar held at the Ridgemont Hotel in San Francisco in the summer of 1993.

Prior to this meeting I had a very powerful meditation experience while listening to a tape called "Enlightenment" that had been written, performed and produced by Rama and his band Zazen. Because of the meditative experience, I harbored very high expectations about meeting Rama, but meeting Rama that night far exceeded any expectations I could possibly have imagined.

I arrived at the Ridgemont Hotel with my girlfriend, who later became my wife. The banquet room was large and the elaborate walls were bright gold and white. In addition to the 30 or so dinner tables, the hotel staff set up a small stage and sound system where Rama was to sit and give his seminar. One of Rama's albums of meditation music was playing

113

over the sound system. Around 300 people were in attendance, dressed in sharp tuxedos and attractive dresses. My guess is that most of the people in the room were around 18 to 29 years old. Rama had not arrived yet so we sat at a table and started making small talk with the people sitting close to us.

The hotel staff started serving dinner that consisted of a green salad with salmon or chicken for the main course. The food was delicious, and I was enjoying the experience of meeting and talking with upbeat and energetic young people. After about 45 minutes we had finished dinner, dessert and coffee. Rama had still not arrived, so I used the opportunity to go to the men's room before the seminar started. I made my way out of the banquet room and started my way down a large hallway when I caught my first glimpse of Rama. He was waking towards the banquet room with two or three other people walking along beside and behind him. Rama and his friends were all sharply dressed in tuxedos. He was extremely tall, and his strides were long and graceful, as if he were gliding. Rama's dark, hawk-like eyes looked straight ahead as he walked. His facial features were sharp and strong, and his tightly curled, long, blond hair was neatly styled. He had a look of confident determination on his face. I felt the desire to look at him some more as he was passing me, but I didn't want to seem rude, so I kept my composure and passed him looking straight ahead but towards the ground. By the time I reached the end of the hall, I started getting a pleasantly strange feeling as if everything was slowing down around me. I felt my awareness shift to a bright and sharp state, and I couldn't repress the urge to look back at Rama. Right before Rama entered the banquet room, he stopped for half a second and looked back at me. I will never adequately be able to describe the look he gave me. It was a look of overwhelming vulnerability and deep love as if he knew who I was. I had an immediate and deep heart-felt response almost as if I had known Rama for a long time. As I turned away to head towards the restrooms I felt a silly feeling of accomplishment. Accomplishment of what? I'm not sure. Some say it is an accomplishment just to be in the same room with Rama.

All night long I had been noticing an increasingly strong sensation of what I can only describe as a living light that filled and surrounded the banquet hall. The sensation like living light reached a zenith with Rama's physical presence. It was not a physical light but more of a bright presence. It seemed to make everything sharper and more animated. The light imparted a timeless feeling in my mind and emotions, and I felt as if I was in another world altogether.

After I got back from the restroom, I saw Rama going from table to table greeting all his guests. Some guests walked up to Rama and asked him various questions, and he talked to them for a time before moving on to greet the other guests.

After about half an hour, Rama walked up onto the stage and took his seat on a shiny black chair set on top of an oriental rug. A yellowish, oriental, paper-screen wall with a print of a fierce dragon on it was set up behind him. He clipped his microphone on to his tie, tapped it to make sure it was on, and greeted everyone with a tremendous smile.

Rama held the group spellbound for hours as he talked about Enlightenment, Buddhism, music, meditation, computer science, martial arts and many other things that he was personally excited about. His enthusiasm and humor were contagious, and he had us all laughing together.

At one point in his talk he told everyone to look at him while he meditated. He said he was going to demonstrate advanced Buddhist meditation. Rama closed his eyes and was silent for only a few seconds before I felt a wave of energy wash over my body. It felt almost like soft and warm electricity. My thoughts immediately slowed to a crawl. One by one, I could sense my thoughts as they floated through my mind. As Rama continued to meditate I lost all notion of time. Light started emanating from him in golden waves. As I continued staring at him, I noticed that he was becoming transparent to my sight! I was trying to make out the lines of the dragon print behind him through his body! Rama had raised my consciousness into such a heightened state that I didn't react to these almost overwhelming experiences with fear, but with an understanding that I was witnessing Rama's world, the world in which miracles were a second-to-second reality.

After a period of timeless time, that could have been between 15 minutes to an hour, he began to speak softly. He was ending the meditation and instructed everyone to quietly bow, and offer the meditation back to the Universe, and take a refreshment break. The look on people's faces after the meditation varied from wide-eyed wonder to slight confusion. "What had other people experienced?" I mused.

I looked over to my friend and she smiled back at me. She seemed to be in an exceptionally good mood. I didn't talk much about what I saw but listened as other people were chatting and laughing energetically. We got up from our table to get some refreshments. As we made our way through the room, I felt as if I were swimming through the air. My body felt powerful and light, and my senses were sharp and alert. I was riding the wave of heightened awareness.

I waited until nearly the end of the break before walking over to meet Rama face to face. I waited my turn as he talked to the other guests also eager to speak with him. When my turn came, I walked up to Rama and blurted out, "Rama, it's good to finally meet you!" His hawk-like eyes were piercing. Without saying a word Rama raised his glass in salute. He had a smirk on his face as he continued to look at me. "Um...Uh, I wanted to ask you a question about meditation," I said kind of nervously. Still without saying a word, Rama gave me a look, which suggested I continue. "Ok, well, I'm currently doing Transmission Meditation," I said, "and I was wondering if it would be OK to do the kundalini Meditation that you teach as well as Transmission Meditation?" Rama answered in a friendly way, "Meditation is like a salad bar. You pick and choose what works for you. If it feels right, then it probably is right." He made a few more comments and recommendations, and by the time our short chat was over my questions were clearly and precisely answered. I felt nothing from him except a desire to teach. I thanked him and walked off to find my friend.

I found her sitting at our table, so I joined her and waited for the second half of the seminar to begin. Rama reseated himself and once again entertained and inspired the crowd with his humor and wit. He took a lot of questions from the group and answered them all with a clarity and thoroughness that I had never witnessed before. By the end of the night, Rama announced that he would be accepting new students for a limited time, but that there was an application process. I didn't have to think twice about what I wanted to do. I was so thankful that I had a chance to apply to study directly with Rama that my mind raced with excitement. Rama wrapped up the night by impressing upon all his guests to be extremely careful going home, and then he wished us all well.

As we left the Ridgemont Hotel, I felt like I was walking on the moon. Any trace of anxiety or fear I had about Rama was replaced with a feeling of unlimited possibilities and a sacred feeling of returning home.

This was the first of many magical nights of Enlightenment that I would directly experience with Rama.

Tributes

My encounters with my teacher, Rama, which were usually conversations, transpired within the most subtle and exquisite, multifaceted, nonlinear, timeless planes of awareness, and as such, are very difficult to capture into words.

In order to be able to talk to Rama, he raised your attention to a compatible level. Thus, your conversations transpired in other dimensions, other planes; you emerged altered, yet not always exalted. Like Krishna, Rama was considerate of his student and concealed his true nature. He could be so easy to be with that you forgot whom you were talking to because it felt so natural. Yet you could make critical errors from this point of view. The reality is that any mental or physical interaction with an Enlightened Being is a psychically charged exchange that accelerates your own tendencies and empowers your current state of mind, for better or worse.

When you were with Rama there was an absence of worldly emotion, and there was such peace. He glowed with genuinely unpretentious eminence and childlike innocence; his presence a shiny mirror in which you saw your own infiniteness. His extraordinary neutrality had a totally singular vibration. It stilled your thoughts. When you stepped into his radiant aura, you felt a little bit of Enlightenment. The refinement, elegance and clarity of this mental state led to totally different views of reality, which seemed to match the elevation of your spirit. The transition was seamless.

Somehow you would know things. Solutions would appear; ideas would blossom. You would feel happy, but it was not ordinary happiness: it was multidimensional. Your heart would smile. You would feel tuned and streamlined, pulled together. You would intuitively understand more than you ever had before, and you would be excited. Life seemed good and wholesome somehow; you would be up for it and in harmony with it.

Rama was also the funniest individual I've ever encountered. His humor was extraordinary because his mind ranged far beyond human limits and wove intricate mental mandalas and maps that defied prediction. His discourses and antics were utterly spontaneous; I have never seen him use a single note. He could be shockingly irreverent, stupendously silly, and mischievous, but never nasty. He often used humor when his students were being "too heavy" in spirit.

117

It was exceedingly difficult to come to terms with who or what Rama was. His actions, presentations, responses, and essence were of another order. He could not be manipulated. He would not tolerate fawning, worship, weakness, greediness, ego, pushing out, pushing in, sexual games, or emotional displays. This required the student to control human tendencies to an incalculable degree. Rama may have completely ignored you, or responded to you in an enigmatic way that you could ponder for years. Yet you had a consistent sense of wonder, delight, trust and intimacy.

Then there were the phenomena, first of which, perhaps, was that your own comments or actions may have emerged quite differently than you had planned. Sustaining your end of an interaction under the scrutiny of his mind, while perhaps observing astonishing visual effects or experiencing profound inner perceptions, created surprising results. This, of course, was the mystery and the challenge. His perfect awareness was too much for the human mind to comprehend. You had to transcend those boundaries to begin to try to understand who he was. I can conceive of no greater motivation.

As Rama's student, I lived in a magical world, sheltered from much of the pain of everyday life in the beauty of Rama's aura. The magic became the norm, and I soon forgot what the ordinary world was like without him. Not only did I forget, but I also came to take for granted this wonderful life that I had. Rama's energy provided a safety net, and things came much more easily. I was able to learn much more quickly, and rapidly progress in my newly found career of computer science. I learned to be less attached and much more fluid in how I lived my life. Rama was my teacher and my inspiration.

Now, although Rama is gone from this physical world, I feel his presence more than ever. It is there all the time, this presence. I only have to think of him. Rama was the physical embodiment of Enlightenment, and he can be felt everywhere and in everything, not just in his music and his books and the memories of my experiences. It brings me great joy and comfort to feel him still in my life.

He is tall, strikingly beautiful and you know when he arrives. I do not mean that heads turn when he walks into a room, although they do. Nor do I mean that a hush falls over the crowd and then they begin to murmur with anticipation, although it does. I mean that the building vibrates a bit, the air shimmers like the air low off a hot desert road. I mean that the sky brightens, the mood shifts, the whole world changes when he is near. Everyone notices that change, and that is why they fall silent, and turn to see and murmur. He is magnetic and you find yourself wanting to be near him, yet the crowd parts to allow a huge amount of space through which he passes. He smiles, as if he knows an incredible secret. Everyone smiles back. Everyone. As he walks through the room, the wave of giddiness moves behind him gently like the wake of a swan, growing in ripples. He is my teacher. He is Rama.

My teacher, Rama, was a magical being, an enigma whose presence was so quietly breathtaking, it silenced the mind. His extraordinary perception enabled him to see the divine in his students. He ached for our own awakening and would stop at nothing, even death, to advance our self-discovery.

Rama was not necessarily nice: he was accurate. This approach was a jolt to my Western sensibilities. I didn't come to trust or love him for a long time. I was drawn to study with Rama because he simply made more sense than anyone I had ever heard. Never using notes, his words were clear and lucid verbal expressions of understandings and perspectives of my own mind and my deepest feelings. Being with him was like coming home.

Rama was a hard teacher, and he raised the bar of his expectations constantly. Yet all of us who studied with Rama, who withstood the rigors of his training, completed the challenging tasks he assigned, and learned to adapt to change, found ourselves on a journey of incredible personal development. By giving us the example of his impeccable standards, and bathing us in golden light while splitting our sides with his humor, in spite of our doubts and negativity our lives were transformed. As our consciousness expanded through Rama's methods, we were able to accomplish amazing things on the material plane while transcending ourselves through wondrous meditations and powerful spiritual epiphanies. These ongoing experiences are bona fide miracles through which I have come to believe in Enlightenment and recognize my teacher as its divine emissary.

In my heart, in life or in death, Rama will always be my teacher, my light and my world.

When Rama meditated, his body turned gold and rays of golden light emanated from him in all directions. This soft golden light of Enlightenment would fill the entire auditorium in which we were sitting. It would pass through my body in waves of bliss. Every emotional and mental impurity would be washed away in this light. My thoughts would cease and my mind became still. For days and weeks after meditating with Rama, the outside world would appear much more bright. As I walked through familiar surroundings, I noticed that I perceived the world differently. I was able to look at the world in a more encompassing, less personal way and absorb much more of its sound, taste, color, and feeling.

Rama's worldly life was a testimony to his Enlightenment. In him, life's most noble qualities were combined in full abundance. He acted perfectly in every situation without any self-consciousness. To spend just ten minutes with him was to participate in an exciting play that made you appreciate how beautiful life is at every moment. His eyes flashed with bright inner illumination, instantly spotting the significant in every moment. It was a joy to sit next to him or walk beside him and feel the pure energy of his aura. Any mundane act he engaged in was fascinating to watch because of the power and grace of his movements. No words or pictures will ever convey the magic of what he was like.

Rama was a very dedicated and inspiring spiritual teacher. His long discourses wove humor, spiritual truths, and worldly ideas into contemporary mandalas of perfect wisdom. They were elevating and funny beyond comparison. Rama was the kindest, most ethical person I have ever known. Every small favor and meager effort was rewarded generously. At all times, he was more concerned about the welfare of others than his own. Despite his illness and busy schedule, he always sensed when a student was in trouble, and would immediately help out. Rama loved to celebrate what was beautiful in life. He would invite us to dinners and trips and throw spectacular parties. Every one of these events was so lavish, magical and bright that it seemed like a dream. All other times, Rama worked at a breathless intensity to run his software companies, design software, offer computer courses, create musical albums, and write books. He encouraged us to approach our own lives in a similar sophisticated way: to develop our minds and career, work hard, and to rejuvenate our spirits by focussing on and celebrating the bright side of life.

Perhaps more than anything, Rama was a warrior. If you wanted a spiritual teacher who only told you what you wanted to hear, Rama was not the teacher for you. If a student lacked self-control, Rama would insist on improvement. Rama would first point out an error by giving the offending student a certain cool glance. Usually one such glance would suffice to correct the problem. If the situation persisted for a while, and if the student was worthy, Rama would finally publicly upbraid him or her with a torrent of the sharpest, ego-crushing criticism. After experiencing such a torching, some students would decide to leave the program. Those who had the strength to accept the criticism and build improvement in their lives based on that criticism became much happier and wiser as a result. The worst thing that Rama could do to you was not to yell at you, but to ignore you.

Enlightenment was manifest as a Buddha in our midst, right here in America in the 1990's, but few people "got it". Rama's Enlightenment did not have to be accepted on faith, unlike the doctrines of many traditional religions. The golden light that radiated from Rama in meditation, the precious light that is discussed in all of the ancient holy scriptures, was in no way difficult to discern; its magic could be seen and felt by anybody.

Once when Rama and I were watching a sunset together, he became very quiet as the sun was making its final exit into the sea. As darkness descended, he remained silent, and I watched his face for a sign of when I should speak. And I noticed a terrible sadness, a terrible reality, what looked to be the troubles of the whole world gathered in the silent and stern lines of his countenance. And yet his eyes gazed at the same time so far beyond this world. It seemed that all of the world's sorrows were being mixed and balanced and purified in some kind of mysterious alchemy, just as he sat and meditated. Finally, after it had become completely dark, he stood up and stretched, and we walked slowly back. What occurred during these 'transactions with the Universe' that Rama had on a regular basis? We cannot know. But for many years, Rama entered into the ecstatic trance of Enlightenment on a regular basis. He was beyond life and death, beyond the body and mind, and had merged himself with a greater reality.

Rama's Etiquette

I was waiting on the dock for Rama's dive boat to come in. He had gone off with his best dive buddy on a special excursion, where they were probably diving to depths far beyond standard recreational limits. Rama was an avid diver with a professional rating and was always experimenting with new equipment and pushing the limits of his physical capabilities. I can't explain why he did this, but it seemed that everything that he did, whether it was meditation, business, or scuba diving, he did with a profoundly uncommon level of dedication and commitment.

As Rama's boat came into view, I relaxed in the sunshine and tried to predict what he might say when he got off the boat. Perhaps he had exceeded his personal maximum depth, or maybe he had seen a shark or an eagle ray. On one occasion he got off a dive boat with a new idea for a software company that had occurred to him somewhere beyond the depths of 200 feet of seawater!

The boat pulled up to the dock and the dive master jumped off the boat to secure the bow. Almost immediately, Rama jumped off and grabbed the second rope, to secure the stern. Within a few seconds the boat was secure, and other divers began climbing off the boat with their gear, and headed for the rinse tank. But Rama stayed by the dive master, and waited for everyone to get off the boat. Then he and the dive master started hoisting all the empty tanks onto the dock, working in an easy rhythm together, without speaking.

When they were finished unloading the heavy 80 cubic foot tanks onto the dock, Rama finally got his own dive bag and lugged it over to the rinse tank. Everyone else was already headed to the bar or to their hotel rooms for a freshwater shower. Rama smiled broadly at me from behind his mirrored sunglasses as he dunked his gear in the rinse tank. He really seemed happier at that moment than I had ever seen him. I watched him and thought about how naturally and automatically he looked for the work that needed to be done, and immediately lended a hand. He was that way in every aspect of his life, and I think this must be what made him so happy.

Once I was talking to Rama on the phone after not having seen him for a few months. We were winding down the conversation, and I was getting ready to hang up.

"Is there anything else?" Rama asked in a tone that suggested he knew there was something I should tell him.

A little light went on in my head. "Oh yeah," I said, suddenly remembering how much my back had been hurting during the last couple weeks. "I got an injury in my back during martial arts, near my—"

"I'll see what I can do," Rama said. Before the words were out of his mouth, I could feel a concentrated ball of energy probing my back for the problem. It found the injury and went into it. My pain immediately melted. I felt a warm glowing light, concentrated in the area of the injury, emanating throughout my body. I spent the rest of the evening pain-free, feeling very grateful to know Rama. As expected, I was completely healed within a few days.

When we were first beginning to study with Rama, a number of fellow students and I noticed that there would almost always be rain on the day before Rama gave a seminar. It didn't matter where the seminar was going to be—San Francisco, Los Angeles, New York, or the desert—wherever the seminar was going to be, it would rain the previous day. It spooked me at first, but later I think we all came to take it for granted.

One day I was hiking alone on Mt. Tamalpais in Marin County, California, under a beautiful, clear sky. I was wandering about the paths, enjoying the scenery and the air, when I suddenly realized that Rama was scheduled to hold a lecture the next evening.

"Funny," I thought to myself, "it hasn't rained today."

Within minutes, a monstrously large, dark cloud rushed in from the ocean and swallowed the sky. The rain came. I was soaked to the skin, searching an hour for my car, because I couldn't see through the rain.

I had many embarrassing moments with Rama, but this one was the worst. I was sitting on a chartered airplane next to Rama, and I was feeling more than a little uptight. When we hit some turbulence, I threw up all over the floor.

Hurriedly, I went to the back of the plane to get something to wipe up. When I got back to my seat, Rama was cleaning up the mess. Horrified, I said, "Please don't clean up after me!"

Rama said, "That's what I do. I clean up after my students' messes."

I realized that time and time again that Rama, as my teacher, took care of every single little detail for me, to help me to reach Enlightenment. His selflessness that day showed me his unending love and dedication to every one of his students. On every level, Rama was happy to assist his students — to find new jobs, improve their karma, meditate better, and generally teach them how to be happy, successful, and self-confident.

One time during the 80's I helped out at a Zen seminar that Rama held at a Unitarian Church in Boston. Rama liked this church a lot as it had been around awhile, and he had told us that people like Emerson and other Transcendentalists had used it in the past. It had a really cool-looking organ, and it was always a friendly place for us.

At this seminar, there was an old Irish cop who was working security. He watched us cleaning the church before the seminar was to start. He looked like he was curious about this whole Zen thing, and he seemed like the kind of guy who would describe it later in the week to his friends at a pub over some beers, how he'd worked at a Zen seminar. He seemed like he approved of us and our cleaning. I chatted with him a little bit, and he asked me how long the seminar would go. I told him about three hours, and he asked me why it was going to be so long. I explained there would be music and meditating, and there would be a break and part of the time Rama would be talking. He liked the part about the break as he thought three hours was a long time for someone to have to talk. I was very struck by this. Most of the people were coming to the seminar for what they could get out of it, and here he was thinking about what it was like for Rama!

The seminar went fine, and at the end of the evening, Rama thanked the people who had worked. He looked very tired, as if he was doing the correct etiquette by thanking us in spite of his exhaustion, but he was obviously completely spent. We filed out to go home. Just as I was leaving the church, something made me turn and look back.

I watched the Boston cop have an encounter with Rama. It looked like something deep inside the cop was bringing him forward to say to Rama, "I'm so glad I got to meet you." I could sense things from his past lives were propelling him to have this moment with Enlightenment, and this might be all he would get in this lifetime, just this one moment. There was a real sincerity about him as he spoke to Rama. I watched Rama drop all his tiredness, instantly brighten and give him a great, momentous smile. "Thank you for helping," Rama said enthusiastically, beaming light at him. The light went into the cop.

It was a simple, quiet moment, but it really touched me watching Rama be so impeccable with this cop, so he would have a special moment with the world of Enlightenment.

When I worked with Rama on software development and he wanted to talk with me, he would usually page me on my SkyTel pager. He would always leave a phone number where I could call him back immediately, rather than leave me a voice message. This way I could get his number off the pager, call him right back, and we would often be talking less than a minute after I received the page. It was efficient, as we both traveled a lot. But sometimes he would page me when I couldn't get to a phone fast enough to catch him. This was always disappointing because I really looked forward to and enjoyed his calls.

One night in 1996 I was driving home on the New York State throughway when my pager went off. It was really late, about 2:00 a.m., and I didn't have a phone in my car. It was unusual for Rama to page me at this hour so I was afraid it was something really important. I pulled off at the next exit and started hunting for a pay phone. There weren't any businesses around, just a closed gas station that was under construction. But I spotted a pay phone to one side where a rutted dirt road led to a parking lot for the tractors and forklifts that would be cranked up the following morning.

I prayed that the phone was working. I glanced at the number on my pager in the dim light of my Honda's interior globe and got out of the car. I grabbed the receiver and breathed a sigh of relief as the dial tone banged loud and clear into my left ear. I punched in the calling card sequence, and then Rama's number. A little out of breath, he answered the phone in about five rings.

"Hi Rama."

"Hi kid. How are you doing?"

"I'm good, Rama."

"So I wanted to wish you a happy birthday."

"Wow, thanks Rama." It was my thirty-eighth birthday, but I really don't pay much attention to my birthdays, and I was surprised that he knew about it.

I looked up at the sky. It was late November and the sky was absolutely stuffed with stars. It was a moonless, clear night, and I was shivering a little, standing on the sloping dirt by the pay phone. But the stars were so clear and beautiful I couldn't stop staring at them.

"You know, we've known each other for a long time," Rama said slowly. His voice seemed to be filled with mystery, it sounded far away, dramatic, like Rod Serling on The Outer Limits. "You and I are old friends. We go way back, farther than you think."

I really didn't know what to say. I continued looking at the stars. My love for Rama was filling my chest and making me light-headed. The stars were literally bursting with light. I seemed to be soaring up into them. I wasn't cold anymore, and the crummy gas station had become a place of brilliance as my mind soared and danced in the heavens.

"Cool," I said, "I didn't know that."

"Happy birthday, kid. A very happy birthday to you."

"Thanks Rama."

"No sweat. Go home and get some sleep."

It was the best birthday present I had ever received.

It was late afternoon on a suburban February Sunday. I was feeling blue and frustrated with my physical life. It was as if nothing would budge. I had been trying to find a new job for several weeks, and it seemed that whatever tack I took, I was running into a brick wall, and was starting to get down on myself. I decided to go to the nicest grocery store I could think of to purchase some happy organic food. Somewhere in the back of my mind I was hoping I would run into Rama, since he always had a way of lifting my spirits and always had good and practical advice.

As I was driving on the country road toward the store, I had a strange sensation at the top of my head, which I can only describe as something like a radio-signal reception. I thought I must have been imagining it, so I ignored it.

I leisurely strolled up and down the track-lit aisles, picking out anything I thought would cheer me up, including bright, perky fruit, and fresh flowers. As I was getting some bagels out of the freezer, I saw out of the corner of my eye a very tall man with curly blonde hair and dark sunglasses walking with a seemingly nonchalant gait down the aisle. I took an immediate double take, almost giving myself whiplash as I turned around completely to look again in no subtle way. Somewhere in that split second, I tried to tell myself that it was impossible...what would Rama be doing in frozen foods?

He turned around, mocking surprise, and smiled. I must have been standing there with my jaw wide open. Although I was blushing terribly, we had a really nice conversation in which he indeed brightened my day. He reassured me that I was doing well, and that I was picking up some ideas about myself that were not true. He cleared up some doubts I had as to whether there was any tension between us, and gave my self-confidence a real boost. About a week later I landed a new job, which was a pay increase for me and a real positive move for my career and my self-esteem.

I found out later that he had been extremely ill for that entire month, and yet had responded to my somewhat unreasonable needs without regard to how he was feeling. He always did things like that for people he cared about.

At one seminar, Rama showed us films of scuba diving in the Caribbean. He explained why it was important not to touch the delicate sea life when you were scuba diving. He said, "Look, but don't touch. That's my greatest teaching about life." I try to apply this teaching in my daily meditations.

One day Rama brought in a group of Judo specialists to give a presentation to two or three hundred of his students. The Judo teacher I remember only as "Sensei Lenny". Sensei Lenny had lost a leg in an industrial accident, putting an end to a very successful career as a tournament competitor. Rather than giving up on life, he went on to teach kids Judo with the same level of dedication he had previously used for preparation for tournaments. Over the years he had consistently produced Olympic-class competitors. Hearing this story increased my understanding of what being a true martial artist was about.

At the end of this demonstration, Rama asked me to come up on stage. As I did, he indicated to the audience that I had trained in Karate for many years. He also explained that in this world today, there really are Ki Masters. There really are people who can access, store, and then direct energy in such a fashion as to completely disable opponents, with only minor physical contact.

Rama asked me to assume a solid stance. He then put an open palm on my forehead, over my third eye, and instructed me not to let him push me down. If you have ever had a student-teacher relationship bound by Oriental etiquette, you would realize that I was in prickly situation. Etiquette requires that the student never bring up his or her will in direct opposition to the teacher. This is not a moral issue nor is it an arbitrary rule — to directly oppose one's teacher essentially stops the educational process. Rama gave me a physical shove, and I staggered back. He said, "No, you're not fighting me. Do it again." This time I really scrunched down and gave him quite a strong stance. He shoved me, and I again staggered back. He then said, in a stronger and more commanding voice, "No, you're not fighting me. Do it over."

I was getting annoyed.

I knew in my heart that if I chose to fully resist him, he would not be able to push me down. This would result in my embarrassing my teacher in front of a large crowd. On the other hand, if I did not give him full effort, he seemed determined to push the matter, quite publicly. The absurdity of the situation pushed me across a line. In my mind I said, "To hell with it," and decided to let him embarrass himself in front of his students.

131

What happened next is very difficult to describe.

Rama put his hand on my forehead and blasted me with kundalini (energy). At that point the continuity of my attention field fragmented and took on three separate existences. By that I mean I have three separate remembrances of the event, although logically they must have all occurred at the same time.

One "remembrance" consists of me standing before Rama and becoming very centered as he put his hand on my third eye. I resisted with all my will to keep from being blown over backwards. At some point, however, a circuit blew out in me - it felt like a circuit breaker in my will popped. My body leaped horizontally into the air and I remember seeing my left hand flopping in uncontrolled spasms out of the corner of my left eye. I hit the mat and instantly bounced back up staggering backwards on my heels with my eyes as big as saucers. I was in an extremely high state of attention afterwards.

Another "remembrance" of this same event is quite different. I was blown down in three separate pieces. The first piece to go down was an outer "me" that was worn and damaged by the abrasiveness of the world. It was like a layering of skin that was dry and scaly and very tired. This left the next layer of "me" still standing. It was very shiny, glowing, and energetic, with the freshness of a newborn baby's energy. The contrast between these two layers was striking. Then this second layer was blown over leaving something standing that, to this day, I cannot assemble in my memory. I cannot describe it, but some aspect of myself was still upright. This third layer was then also blown over, and I was completely on the floor.

The third "remembrance" of this event is also quite distinct from the first two. After he put his hand on my third eye, I was instantly blown into a state of existence that I have no recollection of ever having been in before, yet it had a familiarity about it. It was a state in which everything that I have ever known as me or not-me no longer existed. I was actually surprised that "I" still existed. All other states of mind that I can remember have reference points built into them; however, this had none. Yet there I was, and I was definitely having a good time.

From the perspective of combat, I had been utterly incapacitated (in a very friendly way, of course) for about thirty seconds. Rama later confided that he could safely do this with me because my subtle physical body was "very dense" and because I had meditated with him for several years. He said that if he had blasted one of the Judo kids with that much energy, the kid would have lost his or her mind.

I started martial arts training when I was 16 at a studio run by Chuck Norris. Encouraged by Rama to pursue excellence in martial arts, I continued, branching out. Some of the styles I have practiced over the years are Tang Soo Do, Kung Fu, Muay Thai, Tae Kwon Do and Brazilian Jujitsu. It was exciting to excel at something that Rama also enjoyed. My practice of martial arts has resulted in many positive advancements such as increased awareness and focus, storing more power in the naval center, keeping in good physical shape, and self-confidence.

I had sparred in many semi-contact tournaments, but felt I needed to prove myself in full-contact competition. As a black belt, I decided to fight in an Oyama karate semi-knockdown tournament. The competitors were a lot younger and faster, but I was competitive and learned a humbling lesson in the process. I did not have experience at properly blocking lower kicks to the calves and inner thighs, and as a result, I took a beating. I did not properly prepare for this style of fighting, and knew that there might not be second chances in actual situations on the street. I later learned how to properly block lower kicking strikes. I was further inspired to train in other areas of weakness, such as ground grappling. I always felt encouragement and help from Rama in all of my training.

I remember unexpectedly seeing Rama at a movie theater showing "Mortal Kombat". The fighting scenes were quite vivid and exciting with the enhanced energy from Rama. Later in the evening, he was walking down the center aisle and he gave me a thumbs-up gesture. It was very exciting to have this brief moment with him.

I feel lucky and blessed to have shared a part of the martial arts mindset with Rama, as I have prepared myself over the many years of training. Rama continues to be my inspiration for everything I do in my life.

When I first met Rama, I looked like a hippie. I was a martial artist, but I didn't want anyone to know. I was secretive about my martial arts training because I thought that it made me less spiritual. I thought that being a warrior was too violent, and not a spiritual pursuit. I was having an internal conflict because of my love of martial arts and my love of spirituality — I thought there was a dichotomy between the two.

One day I was having lunch with one of Rama's senior students, and she was talking to me about how to be a warrior. She said, "When you get a black belt, you'll understand." I looked her straight in the eye and responded, "I already have a second-degree black belt." Her mouth dropped open in shock — I had hidden that side of myself too well.

Studying with Rama taught me that this internal conflict that I felt was not a necessary conflict. Rama was a great warrior. The warrior path is the spiritual path for me — they are one and the same.

My favorite martial arts story about Rama was told to me by an eye-witness and then later confirmed to me personally by Rama.

Rama was standing outside of a closed Mexican restaurant late at night, on a deserted rural road in New Mexico, talking to a small group of students. As they were conversing, a male Native American in his late twenties, approximately six feet tall and two hundred pounds, approached in a very agitated state of mind. From the way he carried himself, he appeared to have military or martial arts training, and "moved in", leading with his left side. His right hand was concealed, making it unclear if he possessed a weapon. He appeared to be slightly drunk.

As he closed in, yelling about the condition of his people, Rama stepped before him and said, "I am sorry about how you have been treated, but I had nothing to do with it." He then looked his opponent directly in the eye and in a strong tone of voice said, "I am going to give you something very powerful." The young man faltered, noticing that Rama had his hand concealed in a back pocket. He asked, "What is it...a knife?" Rama replied, "No, it's more powerful than that." The young man asked more intensely, "Is it a gun?" Rama replied even more strongly, "No, its more powerful than that." His opponent asked in an even more aggressive tone, "Well, what is it then?" Rama slowly removed his hand from his pocket and gave the young man a one-hundred dollar bill. The young man, after a brief hesitation, broke down into tears.

Conclusion

In the study of Buddhism, Rama repeatedly told us to ask ourselves, "Is this what I really want to do?" One time he even asked us to tell him what we would do if we had only six months to live.

Thus, although most people typically view their death as a remote experience that will happen in the distant future, this was not my case. And while the events of a near death experience were unexpected, I was neither surprised nor thrown off balance by the fact that death appeared to be imminent. And when given the choice of either living or dying, I had to pause to feel which situation my inner being would prefer, as I felt either was OK. I can only attribute facing death calmly to studying Buddhism and meditation with Rama.

In the year prior to my experience, I began to have the feeling that I would not be in this world much longer. Since I was approaching the age at which my mother had suddenly died, I discounted the feeling, thinking it was possibly a programmed feeling resulting from my mother's death. But when Rama asked me to move from Boston to Westchester, New York, it reaffirmed my feeling that I might not have much longer to live as I felt he wanted me closer so he could watch over me. As a result, the event that occurred was not really unexpected.

On March 20, 1996 I got up at my normal 6:00 a.m. I didn't feel well. It felt like I was getting a migraine which I hadn't had since college. I showered and sat to meditate, but the meditation did not appear to be happening. I just couldn't get my normal focus. After a while, I thought maybe a workout would help. (Normally I did a series of push ups, sit ups, kicks, blocks and punches that took 20 minutes.) I put on my workout shorts and started doing push ups. Normally I did 100 every morning, but my left arm didn't have the strength to support my weight. I moved on to the other exercises and noticed that my left leg was also weak and lacked normal coordination. At this point, I realized I was sick and felt that it would be better to rest, so I went back to bed.

I slept for two hours and woke up feeling no different. My left leg and left arm were weak and slightly numb and now my left peripheral vision was dim. At this point, I realized, I needed to get help, so I called my business partner and asked him to call Rama. When I told him my symptoms, he reminded me that Rama always told us to get medical help when necessary and said he thought he should get me to a hospital. I gave him directions to my apartment in Pleasantville and he was there in a half an hour. At this stage, my left leg was not strong enough to support my weight. I put my left arm around him and leaned on him to walk to his car. When we got to the Mt. Kisco hospital, I again needed his help to walk into the emergency room.

I was given a bed in the emergency room. Two doctors came in and examined me. They asked me a number of questions about my drinking habits as well as what I had been drinking the day before. (I rarely drink anything alcoholic and had not been drinking the day before.) They said they were putting me on an IV and were ordering some blood tests from the lab. They went away. A nurse came, started the IV and left. A lab tech came, drew several tubes of blood and left. My business partner sat in a chair a few feet from the bed, but we talked very little. Although hospital emergency rooms are notoriously crazy places, it seemed very quiet.

I realized for the first time that this was a life-threatening situation and that my life might be ending. I started to review my life very intensely. I saw that through studying with Rama, I had accomplished what I had come to do. As a result, if I did die -- it would be OK. But I also saw that there were people on this earth that I loved and young friends I wanted to help. So it would also be OK to live.

One of the doctors came back and said, "You probably wouldn't be surprised if I said the word 'stroke'." I said, "No," as I had thought this might have been what had happened. By now, my whole left side was partially paralyzed. The doctor said that I would be moved to a private room in the hospital in a couple of hours, as soon as a room was available. My business partner again called Rama with this news. When he came back from the phone, my business partner said that Rama would be by to see me the next day. He stayed with me until I was moved to a private room.

In a couple of hours, two orderlies came with a stretcher, put me on it, and rolled me to a room on the third floor. I was surprisingly happy. Rama was obviously putting energy through me to help me deal with the situation, but I was not alarmed as I knew that whatever happened was going to be OK. Once in my room, I called my sister, my son, and some friends to let them know what had happened and that I was all right.

I was in the hospital for a week. Rama came to see me in the afternoon of the second day. When he came in, one of his younger female students was there, visiting me. She looked at him and asked, "Should I leave now?" Rama responded with the question, "Have you been here for a while?" When she said yes, he said, "Yes, he and I need to talk." She left, and he sat down in a chair at the foot of the bed. In order to sit up, I had the head of the bed raised as high as it would go with pillows behind my back.

Rama gazed at me. He said there had been some damage, but he could heal it if I wanted to stay in this world. He said that if I was ready to leave, he had a nice world for me and I had friends there. He spoke with the deepest love and kindness. I didn't answer immediately. While it felt OK to die, there was a small uncertainty in me as to what would happen and also a small fear of dying. Rama saw that and said gently, "Dying is like walking into another room."

"It feels OK to die," I replied, "but it also feels OK to live." Then I paused for a moment to feel what my inner being really wanted to do, and a voice came out of me from deep inside that said, "I will stay."

After several moments, I added, "Rama, I like these kids; they have heart." I was referring to his younger students.

Rama agreed. I said that I would like, if possible, to help with some of the younger students, and I would like to help him in one of his companies. We talked for a few minutes about this and in a while I said, "Rama, to be honest, I don't understand Enlightenment, but I understand freedom and helping others gives me the closest thing to freedom that I know of." He answered, "Hey, this is Rama, you don't have to tell me that. I see all of your past lives and everything you've ever done."

"Rama, nobody here knows who you are," I said, "You are Krishna." "In incarnate form," Rama answered, correcting me.

"With your level of sensitivity, how can you deal with this world?" I asked. "I'm detached," he said. He then told me to sit back, relax and look at him. "As there is a very slight chance that another stroke could occur," he said, "We can't take any chances. I'm going to set your transit to the next world to ensure you get where you're supposed to go if another stroke happens."

I leaned back against the pillows on the bed and looked into his eyes. I was filled with joy, serenity and an ethereal calm. After a couple of minutes, he said, "It is done." With that, he said he had to go, as he had some people to meet in one of his companies. He stood up slowly and left.

Although I didn't realize it at the time, Rama had raised my level of attention an incredible amount and transferred a significant amount of energy to me in those few minutes. During my stay in the hospital and for few weeks afterward, my spirits were incredibly high.

I found out that my stroke was the result of a cerebral hemorrhage. Many people take months to recover from the symptoms of such strokes or never recover at all. When they released me from the hospital, they gave me a walking cane. I hung it on the kitchen door knob, and after using it once, threw it away a few weeks later. My sister offered me the use of her extra bedroom for as long as I needed, but I declined as I felt it would only encourage me to be dependent on others. I lived in an apartment by myself almost a mile from shopping. On Easter Sunday, about six weeks later, I started running again (before the stroke, I usually ran 2 miles a day). And in May, I got a technical consulting contract at the same rate I had before the stroke. My symptoms were almost gone.

About two months after the stroke, I went to see my doctor, and he was an hour late. When he finally arrived, he apologized. He said that he had been at the hospital, operating on a 25-year-old who had been in a car accident and suffered brain damage. When I asked how the kid would fare, he said, "He will be OK. At 25, people are real malleable, not like people our age. Except for you! You bounced back like a 25-year-old. I've never seen anyone like that." I instantly thought of Rama. Not only did Rama heal me, but he always said that when you study with an Enlightened teacher, it's as if you stay at the age of 25, and it's very easy to make changes in your life.

Recently, I have been swimming in the Caribbean (which I had not done before) and achieved a technical consulting rate that is almost twice what I had achieved before. The healing and empowering energies of my teacher are still with me and grow steadily stronger.

Last night I dreamt that I was sitting at an outdoor cafe, puzzling over my life with a furrowed brow. I looked up and noticed a beautiful man walking by me with a hard, leather suitcase in each hand. It was Rama!

"Hey Rama!" I called out. "Where are you going?"

"I'm going on a journey," he told me.

"Can I come with you?" I asked.

"Not now," he answered, "but you can follow me later." Rama asked, "What seems to be the trouble?"

I opened my mouth to blurt out all of the things that I was going through in the huge, recent upheaval of my personal life. Before I could speak, Rama held up both hands to stop me. "Wait," he said, "let me read your Tarot. I have the special set of the Ancient Masters with me," he said with great magnitude.

Rama proceeded to open up one of the suitcases, "Click, click!" He started pulling something out. They were action figures! There were GI Joe figurines, Xena the Warrior Princess, the WWW champions, and others. Rama placed the action figures carefully in a complicated pattern, like the model of a battle, and began to tell me what it represented. "These men and women here, this represents your relationships. It's very important whom you choose to associate with. They either bring you up or bring you down." At the end of the reading, he said, "But you see, these figurines with all of their weapons - there is too much violence here. There is too much violence in the world, and too much violence in your life. But you see that one over there?" He showed the graceful figurine of a woman in robes, alone and off to the side. The image was of grace, beauty, intelligence and humility. "That's you, but you don't know it yet. That's who you really are."

In one fell swoop, Rama packed up the suitcase and stood up to leave. "No, Rama, don't go," I pleaded.

"I'm a traveling man," he responded.

"Don't leave me alone," I begged. "I want to come with you."

"There are endless roads in the universe, and these roads will eventually cross at some point."

I knew that some day I would see Rama again. Suddenly, as if it were a movie, a song started playing in the background. It was the country western song, "On the Road Again". And Rama sauntered off down the road.

In 1997, Rama responded to students who were inspired to teach meditation and Buddhism by providing a special opportunity to receive a teaching empowerment and his blessing to become exoteric teachers. Because Rama believed in a thorough education, he set up a program whereby we were to read 29 fundamental and advanced books from the Buddhist, Hindu, Confucian, and Taoist traditions in a very short period of time. It was not an easy feat to accomplish. For those of us who did complete this task, we had the honor of a special meeting with Rama during the fall equinox on a Caribbean island. Rama had given people empowerments to teach before, but this was special because he revealed to us that night that we would receive a "full lineage empowerment". This meant that the power, wisdom and heart of the complete line of Rama's teachers, and their teachers and every Master in his line of Enlightenment could come through us fully when teaching meditation to others. We did not take this lightly. In fact, we felt very privileged and honored to be given this opportunity and blessing from Rama.

Rama talked to us about his experience teaching meditation. He had devoted his whole life to his students, teaching night after night with unending energy and commitment. He said that we would gain an appreciation of what he had endured in his 25-plus years of teaching. But he also told us that we would experience the unparalleled joy of seeing the positive transformations in peoples' lives just as ours had changed when we took up the practice of meditation and Buddhism when we met him. Rama made it very clear that we would not be representing him when teaching. Instead, we were to use our own experiences and realizations to show people that meditation really works. He explained that teaching is one of the fastest paths to Enlightenment and one of the best ways to, as Rama put it, "give back to the system." He told us that teaching would be our way off of the 'Wheel of Life' that turns ceaselessly and causes us to reincarnate time and time again. At the end of Rama's teaching empowerment, he sent us on our way with these final words, "Whenever you feel confused or unclear, meditate. Whenever you're unable to make a firm decision, wait. And may your journey in teaching, now and in all your incarnations, be bright."

I once had a dog named Magic. I was her second Mother. She lived with me and my two other dogs, Heather and Zuni for about five years. She and Heather were always very bonded. They would play and cuddle together, and Magic seemed to dote on her. They lived many happy years together.

In late 1996, Heather developed an undefined illness, most likely a liver or kidney disorder, and died quite suddenly. Magic was very upset by the loss of Heather and seemed to pine for her. Nothing I did for her after that seemed to make up for her loss. She used to look at me with those big, round eyes of hers as if pleading for something, which I was not able to produce.

About eight months later, Magic developed lymphoma. I found two marble-sized lumps in her throat in early June of 1997, and several weeks later, she was gone. Some people call cancer the disease of sadness, in this case, they may be right.

At the time of the diagnosis it wasn't determined yet if the disease had spread throughout her system, and there was the opportunity to treat her with chemotherapy, giving her perhaps a fifty-fifty chance of survival. Feeling in despair and wanting to save her, I obtained the chemo drugs and took them home, but found that I just could not give them to her. At this point I really was confused as to what to do, and was very torn, torn by what I thought I "should" do, and what I was actually doing.

I needed some spiritual advice.

I had not attended any meetings with Rama for several years but I wrote a desperate note via email, and a friend who was attending a class of his passed my note on to him, telling him of the situation with Magic and my quandary of what to do.

To my astonishment, Rama phoned me the next day while I was at work. The first thing he said was, "Don't do the chemo." Of course I broke down in tears throughout the rest of the conversation. He validated my feelings of not wanting to give her the drugs. He told me to listen to my body: I obviously didn't want to do it. The tests revealed several days later that the cancer had indeed spread throughout her system.

Rama said Magic wanted to go, and that I should just let her go, that I was tough and could handle it. I said sarcastically, "Yeah, well at this rate I'm getting tougher all the time." He said to go through it, and experience it with her. "Well, it sucks!" I said, protesting. "*Tell* me about it," he said, with an edge of commiserating pain in his voice.

He said not to worry, that Magic was going to what he called "The Happy Dog World" and that she would be in good company. "We're all going there," he said. And as if to make sure I heard him, or to drive the idea home, he said it again, "We're ALL going there."

All I could do was to thank him and tell him I loved him. I didn't have anything else to say. I felt no desire to speak about my life to him. I didn't need to. Everything had been said in our conversation regarding the life and death of Magic.

He advised me to get a new dog, a puppy, right away after she passed. He said, "I know you won't want to do it. Just do it anyway. You need that new life. Don't wait. Otherwise you just focus on the loss, the empty space left behind."

A few nights later I had a dream that I was getting out of bed and found Magic in the hallway being sick. I felt repulsion at the illness. I wanted to run away from it, not experience it. I was disgusted by it. But then I felt or heard a voice telling me to, "Just BE with it." And I realized my repulsion was coming from my own fear of illness and death.

From then on I stayed with Magic, held her close, kept her as comfortable as possible, and told her over and over how well loved she was.

During her last night, it was as if Eternity was coming for her in waves, as if she was on a shore and it was inevitable that she would be taken out to sea. The sea always wins. It was just a matter of time. There was also an undeniable presence of Heather around her. I could almost hear Heather cheering her on, "Come on Madgie, come on! It's nice here." I woke up with a start at 2 a.m., and she was gone.

144

Well, I did get that new puppy. I found him a few weeks later and Rama was right about that part. You just have to be with it, be with everything: new life, joy, beauty, loss, illness and ultimately, death. Just go ahead and be with it, because life may afford us little option but to simply accept and learn from our circumstances when we are helpless to change them.

I had a very memorable chance encounter with Rama one evening in December 1997, a few months before he left his body. I was having dinner alone at a popular Sushi restaurant in Greenwich, when Rama walked through the door, came over to my table, and sat down as if we had planned to meet there all along. I was thrilled and also horrified, because I hadn't exactly dressed well for the evening and was not in the greatest state of attention! He made jokes about being surprised to see me, and I lamely tried to explain that I had a ticket for the 8:00 showing of Titanic which was playing down the street. "What a coincidence!" he joked, "so do I!" He said we could go together and ordered some light dinner. We chatted about this and that, and he talked to me about some of the reasons I hadn't been happy lately, things that I needed to address in my personal life to get back on track. When Rama finished his dinner, we left the restaurant and headed over to the theater.

Although Titanic was not exactly Rama's kind of movie, there were a few scenes that he commented on that I will never forget. One of the scenes took place while the ship was sinking, and Jack (the hero) was trapped below deck. His girlfriend goes to find help, and finding no one to help her, she grabs an ax and goes back to save him. By the time she returns to the area where he's trapped, so much water has come in that she has to swim. I asked Rama if he thought someone could really survive a swim like that in freezing water. "No way!" he said, "You'd be dead in a few minutes; this is just for the movie." But then suddenly, in a quiet voice he added, "LOVE can make you do that. If you love something enough, you can overcome incredible things, even things that would normally kill you."

After the movie was over and we were leaving the theater, Rama predicted that it would "make all its money back." I was really surprised, because the theater was practically empty and it was the opening weekend. But of course, he was more than right!

We walked up Greenwich Avenue to the local diner, and on the way, Rama told me that he had rented a house in Switzerland that he hadn't even seen yet because he was so busy. He was light about it, but it concerned me because he seemed really worn out, although he was in good spirits as always! But I had never seen him look more in need of a vacation, so I asked him why he didn't just go. I was serious and insistent, asking the question repeatedly, but he either laughed it off or just seemed annoyed by the question. I dropped it until we got to the diner, but when he mentioned that he had only been sleeping four hours a night, I asked him again. I said quietly, "Why don't you just go? Better a *distant* Rama than a dead Rama." He acknowledged my concern but answered that his students needed him too much and he couldn't just leave them. His tone was loving and wistful, and didn't imply that it was a disagreeable burden to him or even an inconvenience, even though he obviously paid a price in terms of his physical health and well being. Then, sounding a little surprised and even a little offended, he said that the people working in one of his software companies had been telling him the same thing. "I called the other day to invite them out for a movie," he said, "and they said 'Rama, you've been sick. Why don't you just stay home and rest? We can do it some other night.' But *I* knew they needed it; they had been working really hard and they needed a break that night in order to get the software finished. They needed a fun night out with me; they needed the empowerment to push through the next couple of months, because we have a lot to do." Then, sounding frustrated he added, *"None* of you understand! This is what I *do*. I *teach*. I help people with their lives. I take on that responsibility. I won't just *leave.*"

I think that there are two things the world will never understand about Enlightened Masters, and something the general public certainly did not understand about Rama in his lifetime: the unwavering commitment to Enlightenment, and what it takes to live that commitment, every single day of your life.

As Rama said on many occasions, "Enlightenment is not what you think it is!"

One day during a backpacking trip through Central America, I came across a funny-looking man, whom all the locals said was crazy. He walked up to me, and for a short while stared at me very intensely. He then let out a howling laugh and gave me the warmest, sincerest hug, saying to me in Spanish that: "You have a very powerful teacher. You should always love him. Always!"

For more information about Rama:

www.fredericklenz.com

www.himalaya.com

www.americanbuddha.com

www.ramatribute.com

www.zazen.com